Read This (No, seriously)

LSAT is a registered trademark of Law School Admission Council, Inc. (LSAC). LSAC does not review or endorse specific test preparation materials or services. Neither Dan F. Oakes nor Acme LSAT Prep is affiliated with the Law School Admission Council, Inc.

Here's something else about the LSAC: They have some great products and critical information about the LSAT. If you're going to be taking the LSAT, spend a lot of time on their website: www.lsac.org.

This book breaks down LSAT Prep Test 60 (June 2010). It <u>does not include Prep Test 60, nor does it reproduce the questions from Prep Test 60. If you don't have a copy of Prep Test 60, this book will be USELESS to you. Either don't buy this book or (much better) pick up a copy of Prep Test 60.</u>

<u>Why doesn't it include Prep Test 60?</u> Because of the combination of royalty payments AND licensing fees, I would have to raise the price of the book by *more* than you could buy LSAT 60 from on your own. Plus, some of you already have it, in which case ALL of the price increase would be you double-paying for nothing. It's better for you this way.

One great place to get a hold of Prep Test 60 is at Cambridge LSAT, where you can download it instantly to your computer. www.cambridgelsat.com. Another great place is as part of the book "10 New Actual, Offical LSAT Preptests with Comparative Reading™" which is available at the LSAC website, on Amazon, at many if not most Barnes and Noble locations, and in college bookstores. It includes Prep Tests 52-61 (all ten of 'em) for a very low price. Highly recommended.

Excerpts from (in the form of references to) the questions of Prep Test 60 are included in this work are included with the permission of Law School Admissions Council, Inc., Box 2000, Newtown, PA 18940, the copyright owner. LSAC does not review or endorse specific test preparation materials or services, and inclusion of said excerpts does not imply the review or endorsement of LSAC.

Cover photo by Ken Sands.

Contents

Read This	1
Table of Contents	2
How to Use This Book	3
Dedication/Acknowledgements/Inspirations	4
Section I (Logical Reasoning)	6
Section II (Logic Games) — Game 1 (Arts & Crafts Workshops)	45
Game 2 (Six Actors)	54
Game 3 (The Landscaper)	64
Game 4 (Photographers & Writers)	73
Section III (Logical Reasoning)	82
Section IV (Reading Comp) — Passage 1 (New Urbanism)	118
Passage 2 (Animal Communication)	127
Passage 3 (Teatro Campesino)	134
Passage 4 (Law Reform in Australia)	147
Afterward	159
About the Author	160

What This Book is, and How to Use It

What this book *isn't* is an A-Z how-to book on the LSAT. You *will* get a bunch of how-to general LSAT tips scattered through this book, but they're in the context of addressing the specific questions of Prep Test 60. This book assumes (excuse the personification) that you already have some knowledge of the LSAT. So, for instance, when you get to the part that covers the logic games, there's not preparatory "Hey, here's how you diagram and attack a logic game" section; it just dives into the four games that appear in Prep Test 60 and assumes that you're somewhat up to speed.

What it *is* is a breakdown of every question on Prep Test 60, and every answer choice. It's written in an over-my-shoulder approach that puts you in the mind of a knowledgeable LSAT taker. Each question comes with a "Forethoughts" section that describes the thought process that occurs after reading a question (or a Reading Comp passage, or a Logic Game) – what to look for, what to watch out for, etc. Then there's an answer-choice-by-answer-choice breakdown of every question, followed by an "Afterthoughts" section where the most instructive takeaway points are elaborated upon.

The best way (if not the only way) to make good use of this book is to take Prep Test 60. You don't have to simulate full-blown test conditions, but it would be a good idea to put yourself on a timer and do at least one full section at a time. As you take the test, mark the questions that you thought were hard – maybe there were some where you eliminated 2 or 3 answers, but guessed between the remaining 2 or 3. You want to note which questions those are, because if you don't, and you get one of them right, you won't worry about it (and you should). Then check out the questions you missed, the ones that were hard, the games you had trouble setting up or that took you too long…review the writings in here about those questions and games, particularly the answer you chose and the credited answer. See why the right answer is right, or what it is about your answer that could have led you to eliminate it.

Dedication, Acknowledgements, and Inspirations

Dedicated to Shelby Oakes, an extraordinarily supportive and wonderful mother. She was also a heck of a home plate umpire, back in the day.

Acknowledgements (and inspirations) in no particular order:

Felicia Williams at LSAC for helping me to avoid stepping on legal toes as I try to continue to do what I do; Matt Cucchiaro at Campus Prep for turning me loose on countless future law students and trusting me with the freedom to create my own curriculum, being the first person to compensate me for my writing about the LSAT, AND providing a high-quality, low-cost alternative for students wanting to take LSAT prep courses. www.campusprep.org; Morley at Cambridge LSAT (dot com) a great source of info about a lot of stuff, and whose website and books have done great things for students. He's a visionary; The whole gang at Acme LSAT Prep; Marilyn P., a fellow former journalist who will be sworn into the California State Bar in the near future, for being the first person to ask for my help while preparing for the LSAT, telling me how well I explained it, and telling me how much people actually pay for such services. For better or for worse, Little Marilyn, you started all this; Boris M., with whom I once had the following conversation: "What are you doing this weekend?" "I'm taking the LSAT. You should take the LSAT." A few months later, I did. A few years later, I was a lawyer. So there you go; Michael D., who was the first person to pay me full-time to write. Story meeting at the S.R.! That deserves a paragraph break.

Tons of teachers/professors from elementary school through law school. In chronological order: Diane Reed; Debbie Schiller; Dan Heiman; Nancy Rayl; Cornel Bonca (Times a hundred. Seriously); Joanne Gass; Chris Ruiz-Velasco; Sherri Sawicki; Martin Blaine; Irena Praitis; Mary Kay Crouch; Peter Arenella (Times a hundred. Again, seriously. It was a singular honor to learn the law from you); Steven Yeazell; Kirk Stark; Steve Derian; Tony Tolbert; Tom Holm; Sky Moore; and Michael Asimow.

Family: The Oakeses, past & present; the Arendses (and with them, the Turners, Cornwells, & Wards); the Drakes (and likewise Strohmans and Walkers); the Wises.

Friends, Romans, Countrymen, new & old: Cyn – sunshine, friend, Payroll Goddess; Razz, KIT (now KIL); Kip; Jason; Ken "The Sandman"; Maureen & Abbey – so similar, yet so different; Jimmy Q; Chuck "The Big Cat"; John (and by this, I mean Davidson); Beth (and, sure, why not, Glenn); Steve C.; Michelle L.D.M.; Randy S.; the gangs at the Anaheim Bridge Club (but especially Sharon N. and all of the Evanses), the Glendale Regency Bridge Center (but especially Tim Lolli, for putting up with me), Labate's Chess Center, the Magic Café; and Burbank's Open House Toastmasters and Toastmasters for Writers.

And those in various fields whose work I'm a fan of. Greatness, in any field, inspires me: Steve, Bruce, Adrian, Dave, Nicko, and even Janick – Up the irons!; Raymond Carver; J.D. Salinger; while I'm on the subject of writing – John Irving. If you haven't read "A Prayer for Owen Meany," for the love of God, put THIS down and do so at once. The LSAT will still be here when you get back; Dennis Lehane; Michael Connelly; Robert Crais; T. Jefferson Parker; Lee Child; John Cazale; Betty White; Richard Jeni; Rod Serling; John, Terrence, Tony & Bill (saying "Ozzy" would have given it away); Edvard Munch; Salvador Sanchez; Whit Haydn; Bob Cassidy; Shoot Ogawa; Michael Vincent; Dave Wyndorf; Dexter Morgan; Billy Bob Thornton (I still can't see even a little bit of him in Karl Childers); Steve Carell; and Ed Norton (who should have at least 3 Oscars by now. If you're keeping score at home, that's American History X, Primal Fear, and The People v. Larry Flynt (supporting but still)); and BUCKETHEAD.

Sections 1 & 2 from the UCLA School of Law (and selected individuals from other sections and law schools – Jessica H. & Jill F., this means you), but most especially, the inner circle – Zach R., Patrick H., Paul B., Sarah R., Mike "Public Policy" M.

And all of my students, past & present.

Is this section getting long? It's my party; I'll thank who I want to. But, ok...on to the LSAT.

Section 1 (Logical Reasoning)

1. Forethoughts: The prompt warns me that Jim is making an error in his reasoning, so as I read the passage, I'm going to bear in mind that it's flawed. Moreover, I'm told what the flaw is – an alternative explanation ("...fails to consider that"). The premise, which we have to accept, is that the magnet attracted the substance. The conclusion, which we *don't* have to accept, is that it contains iron. The alternative explanation pretty much has to be that the substance had something besides iron that is magnetic. I often restate the argument to myself in a simple sentence, to have a clear vision of it, and I use the formula, "Y is true because of X." That's it; one-sentence argument (whenever possible). Here, that would be, "The substance has iron, because it attached to the magnet."

   (A) Incorrect. This answer choice is irrelevant, because the substance *did* attach to the magnet. That's my "X." This would be a great answer if the substance failed to attach to the magnet and Jim concluded that it therefore *did not* contain iron; then a possible flaw with Jim's reasoning might be that iron is not always attracted to magnets. In other words, it might be a false negative – the fact that something did not occur might not be a 100% indicator of whatever it is that is being tested. In this case, though, we don't have to worry about what it might or might not mean if the iron *failed* to attach to the magnet, because that didn't happen. We need an explanation for X, not an explanation for "not X."

   (B) Incorrect. Similar to (A), this describes a separate, and irrelevant, possibility. Jim is saying that because the magnet attracted the substance, it must be iron. Whether anything else might have attracted the substance is outside the scope of his little experiment. Analogy: I taste a cup of coffee, and it's sweet, so I conclude that the coffee has sugar in it. The fact that other drinks also have sugar in them doesn't hurt my conclusion about the coffee. (What *does* hurt my conclusion about the coffee is that things other than sugar are sweet. See the difference?

   (C) Incorrect. This sounds even more similar to (A) than (B) does. It would be a decent explanation for why the magnet might *not* have attracted the substance, but the magnet DID attract the substance. "Needs to be oriented a certain way" sounds like an excuse a magnet salesman might give for why it didn't work; the problem with it as an answer choice is, the magnet worked just fine.

   (D) Correct. First, it discusses a situation that is consistent with what took place – magnets attracting substances. Second, it undercuts Jim's conclusion by pointing out that it's not *only* iron that magnets attract. So maybe the substance was iron, as Jim thought, or maybe it was one of those other substances – a "possibility" that Jim "failed to consider."

(E) Incorrect. Another off-point choice. The question is what to infer from the fact that one magnet attracted one substance. What other magnets do is irrelevant. The distinction in the passage is only about the fact that magnets DO attract iron – it doesn't matter how strong that attraction is.

Afterthoughts: This question is a great example of two things the examiners love to test: the "alternative explanation" and the conditional relationship. First, the alternative explanation: Jim's flaw was that he concluded that something that *might* have been true *must* have been true. In a nutshell, "Because the magnet attracted the substance, the substance was iron." The question to ask is, "What other reason *might* there have been that the magnet attracted the substance?" Only (D) answers that question – maybe the substance was a magnetic substance other than iron.

Second, even though the words "if" and "then" weren't used, conditional logic was in place. Jim knew that magnets attract iron. His premise was, "If a substance is iron, then a magnet will attract it." (If P, then Q). His flaw was that assumed the converse was true: "If a magnet attracts a substance, then the substance is iron." This is an invalid deduction. Another example: If I'm drinking something and you don't know what it is, you could correctly say, "If he's drinking vodka, then his drink has alcohol," but it would be incorrect to say, "If his drink has alcohol, then he's drinking vodka." Conditional statements are one-way streets[1]; you can't just reverse them. Alcohol is contained in drinks other than vodka – just as magnets attract substances other than iron. Again, (D) cuts to the heart of that logical flaw.

2. Forethoughts: This "method of reasoning" prompt means that the answers aren't going to be about the subject matter, specifically; instead, they'll be worded in very general terms. The best way to evaluate the answer choices will be to look very specifically for content in the passage that matches up to the general terms, e.g. "a generalization," or "a specific example." To help avoid distracting wrong answers, I'm going to try to summarize the passage in general terms before moving on to the answers. The logic of the passage is direct – the book must have been misplaced or stolen, because all of the other possibilities are accounted for: It's not on the shelf, displayed, in use, checked out, or awaiting shelving. In other words, process of elimination.

(A) Incorrect. This answer choice doesn't match the "predicted" answer, so it's an unlikely candidate right away. Sometimes, though, the predicted answer is wrong, so we should consider the answer on its merits. Again, that means checking for the answer's key terms in the passage. For instance, this answer choice refers to "a general conclusion." However, the passage's conclusion is not general; it is *very* specific – it deals with one particular book. This confirms that

---

[1] The exception is an "if and only if" statement; in that case, it works both ways. But those are an extremely small minority of the conditional statements you'll be asked to deal with on the LSAT.

answer choice A is not a good answer. Many LSAT answers and wrong answer choices revolve around the distinction between "general" and "specific" conclusions; it's always a good idea to pay attention to the degree of specificity in the answer choice and see if it describes what's really happening in the passage.

(B) Incorrect. Again, this answer choice does not provide the "process of elimination" idea that we're looking for. It is superficially attractive, because the library's system apparently *did* "fail to control one of the objects that it was intended to control," but looking at the first part of the answer choice, the passage does not isolate "a deficiency in the system." The passage makes a conclusion about what happened to one book; it does not isolate a single deficiency, or even reach a conclusion about the "system." The elements of the system are merely *premises* for the writer's conclusion[2] about one single book.

(C) Incorrect. Another answer choice that doesn't illustrate the process of elimination. (C) refers to a generalization, but the passage does not contain any generalization about lost books ("lost books" being the only think that "most such objects" might refer to). Also, the passage contains no rebuttal to a conclusion about the particular book. The writer is not disagreeing with anyone about the fate of the book Horatio wants; he is simply reaching an independent conclusion.

(D) Incorrect. Another answer choice that ignores the main technique of the passage's reasoning – process of elimination. (D) refers to a "generalization" that is "rejected." That's inconsistent with the passage. As with (C), nobody is providing a different explanation for what happened to the book, so there's nothing to "reject" ((D)) or "rebut" ((C)). Also, there is no generalization that "fails to hold." This answer choice makes it sounds as if the author said that because of the library's system, books cannot be stolen. That would be a generalization that fails to hold in this particular instance. That's not what the passage says, though. The passage does not contain a generalization.

(E) Correct. Right on point. The conclusion of the passage is that the book was misplaced or stolen. How is it supported? The author rules out "other explanations" (in use, checked out, on a special display…) for "an observed fact" (the book is not on the shelf where it's supposed to be).

Afterthoughts: The technique of predicting the answer, although it's not infallible, is extremely useful. It's a useful way to avoid being distracted by wrong answers (in all types of Logical Reasoning questions). The technique of looking for specific terms in the

---

[2] If you're not doing so, you need to be identifying the conclusion of every passage that contains an argument (not all of them do; some are just collections of facts). "Since" is a great word to see in a passage; it indicates that both a premise and a conclusion will appear in the same compound sentence. The premise will be on the same side of a comma as the "since," and the conclusion (in this case, "it must have been…") will be on the other side.

passage to match up to the general terms in the answer choices is the best way to evaluate the answer choices in this type of question. Notice again how directly all of the terms in (E) correspond to the passage, from "The conclusion" to its "support," to the "other possible explanations," to the "observed fact." Every key term in (E) reflects a portion of the passage. Because of the absence of any generalization in the passage, (A), (C), and (D) are not really plausible wrong answers (they all refer to a generalization or a general conclusion). (B) is kind of attractive as wrong answers go. To separate (B) from (E), again, notice that the passage does *not* isolate "a deficiency in the system" ((B)), and also that (B) completely ignores the process of elimination.

3. Forethoughts: I have a conditional premise (If the regulations had been followed, then the sulfur dioxide would have decreased), so I'm absolutely going to focus on the contrapositive and beware of the converse and inverse, the improper deductions. From the statement "If P, then Q[3]" we can correctly deduce: "If not Q, then not P" (contrapositive). We *cannot* properly deduce either "If not P, then not Q" or "if Q, then P" (inverse and converse, respectively). Always be on the lookout for these variations when you have a conditional statement; the examiners *love* to test your understanding of these relationships. In the final sentence, "P" is "the regulations were followed," and "Q" is "the level of sulfur dioxide would have decreased."

I also have a straightforward premise: "The level of sulfur dioxide is higher than it was 10 years ago." Putting the conditional premise into the P/Q formula, this fact about the sulfur dioxide levels translate to: "not Q" (the levels did not *decrease* – they *increased*). This looks like a pure contrapositive setup: Premise: If P, then Q. Premise: Not Q. The conclusion we're looking for almost has to be "Not P," in other words, the regulations were NOT followed. If they had been, the sulfur dioxide levels could not have increased. So my predicted answer is, the regulations weren't followed.

(A) Incorrect. Classic mistaken inference – the inverse. This is "If not P, then not Q," which is not a deduction we can validly draw. The premise is: "If the regulations were followed (P), then the sulfur dioxide levels would have decreased (Q)." That statement doesn't say *anything* about what would happen if the regulations are *not* followed. Maybe the levels would decrease either way. Consider this analogy: I could say, "If John is a doctor, then 1+1 = 2." That's a true statement, but that doesn't mean that if John is *not* a doctor, 1+1 *doesn't* equal 2. Also, the premises pertain to what would have happened in the *past* (the levels "would have decreased"). That does not imply that the same relationship between the regulations and the sulfur dioxide levels will continue into the future.

(B) Correct. First, it's right on point with the contrapositive – the regulations weren't followed, because we know that if they had been, the sulfur dioxide levels could

---

[3] In formal logic, philosophy types use "P" and "Q" in the same way that in algebra, math types use "x" and "y."

not have increased – they would have decreased. Also notice that this answer choice offers a conclusion about the past, which is consistent with the passage's statements about the past (contrast with (A)).

(C) Incorrect. A classic distraction-type answer choice. It mentions all of the relevant terms (regulations, sulfur dioxide levels, decrease...) and has a bit of an offbeat conclusion that might even be true. This inference, though, is not certain from the premises. How do we avoid being trapped by this choice? There are two strong clues. First, nothing in the passage hinges on the *degree* of strength of the regulations. It's about whether the regulations are followed or not – it's binary, like a light switch, not a dimmer. What would have happened if the regulations were followed – yes or no. Not "stronger." Second, (C), like (A), draws a conclusion about the future. This is unjustified; the premises only tell us what would have happened in the past.

(D) Incorrect, and wholly beyond the scope of the passage. This is similar to (B) in question #1. The premises involve the pollution that comes from coal-burning power plants. The validity of that conclusion does not depend on whether or not coal-burning power plants are "one of the main sources of air pollution."

(E) Incorrect. There are at least three big problems with (E). Again, it's an answer choice that reaches a conclusion about the future. Second, (E) has another classic "wrong answer" sign – the overstated conclusion. Beware of words like "never," "always," "invariably," "certainly," etc. Even when they're consistent with the argument's reasoning, they're often too definite to be the right answer. One common <u>exception</u> would be a syllogism that is true by virtue of the definitions of the categories, such as: "All Canadians are good hockey players. Bob is a Canadian. Therefore, Bob is certainly a good hockey player." If you're familiar with Venn diagrams, these would be the type where one circle is completely enclosed within another circle. In that case, words like "always" and "definitely" may apply. The key is, the degree of strength of the conclusion can't exceed the degree of strength of the premises.

The third big problem with (E) is that the conditional statement in the passage has clued us in to the strong probability that the correct answer will pertain to whether or not the regulations were followed – a key element of the reasoning that is completely left out of (E).

Afterthoughts: (A) and (C) are the superficially attractive wrong answers. The best way to avoid them is to have a good prediction of what the right answer will look like. That will almost certainly get you past (C), which ignores the question about whether or not the regulations were followed. To distinguish (A) from (B), you need to zero in on the contrapositive and the incorrect inference from the conditional premise (the inverse).

Whenever you see a conditional premise, you have to be thinking in those terms – the contrapositive (valid) and the inverse and converse, which will often be wrong answer choices. Conditional logic is the single most heavily tested concept on the LSAT.

4. Forethoughts: Similar to question 2, this will require understanding the connection between the general terms in the answer choices and the specific terms in the passage. Additionally, because we're looking for the function ("role") of a particular sentence, it's even more important than usual to have a firm grasp of the passage's conclusion, premises, etc., and also to notice any key words that may offer further clues to the roles that various phrases are performing. These types of questions are not inherently difficult, but they require attention to detail and focus on the structure of the argument.

There are some useful "clue phrases" in the passage. First, the phrase that there will be a crisis is preceded by "Some people maintain..." Second, it is immediately followed by, "However..." Clearly, the Ecologist *disagrees* with the prediction about the crisis. The sentence that begins with "However" also provides the basis for that disagreement – the people with whom he is disagreeing are relying on an "unlikely assumption."

- (A) Incorrect. (A) contains nothing about the disagreement that the Ecologist has with the claim at issue. The Ecologist is the only one speaking; essentially, he's having a debate with himself. He brings up the point in order to disagree with it, because he's not only speaking for himself, but he's also playing Devil's Advocate. The right answer will probably reflect this disagreement. Second, and more importantly, (A) *doesn't* follow (directly, anyway) from the claim in the first sentence – it only follows if you add the "incorrect assumption" that no new landfills will open as the currently active ones close.

- (B) Incorrect. (B) definitely misses the mark, and it illustrates the importance of seeking out the passage's conclusion. The Ecologist's conclusion (revealed by the indicator word "therefore") is that the predicted crisis is *unsound*. In other words, the Ecologist concludes that there will *not* be a crisis at all, because new landfills will be built to replace the existing ones.

- (C) Incorrect. (C) is similar to (B) in that it is on the opposite side of the position that the Ecologist is taking. Far from "establishing the truth" of the Ecologist's argument, it actually represents the *false* belief that the argument is attacking.

- (D) Correct. (D) acknowledges the disagreement that the Ecologist has with the "Some people" who are maintaining the excerpted claim. The phrase "cast doubt" is not used in the passage; we have to infer the purpose of the argument from phrases like, "Some people maintain," "However," and "therefore unsound." These are the indicators that the argument "as a whole" is designed to cast doubt on the position that there will be a crisis.

- (E) Just like (A), (B), and (C), (E) incorrectly suggests that the excerpted phrase is consistent with the Ecologist's point. The "crisis statement" *is* a conclusion of the people with whom the Ecologist is disagreeing (based on the limited capacity of the landfills), but that does not make it an intermediate conclusion of the argument. An "intermediate conclusion" provides the basis for a further conclusion. The excerpted statement is not a step *supporting* the Ecologist's main conclusion; it is the completely separate conclusion of the "some people" the Ecologist is disagreeing with.

Afterthoughts: When there are competing arguments in play, be sure to clarify in your own mind which is the position of the main speaker. If you're clear that the Ecologist's position is contrary to the position of "some people," then you'll be able to zero in on the one answer choice that illustrates that disagreement.

5. Forethoughts: To resolve a discrepancy, it's crucial to clearly identify the discrepancy first. I wish I had a dollar for every time a student of mine has missed a "resolve the discrepancy" question after racing to the answer choices before being clear on what the discrepancy was. If you don't know what the apparent discrepancy is, your chances on these questions are pretty much 1 in 5 – a pure guess. An "apparent discrepancy" means that there are two things in the passage that seem to be inconsistent at first glance, but will make sense in light of the correct answer choice. Here, the two things that don't make sense are 1) not many people seem to get disease P in Country X, but 2) the ones who do get it in Country X are much more likely to die than people from anywhere else. So the correct answer should involve both the rate of incidence of the disease in Country X, and the fatality rate from the disease.

- (A) Incorrect. A good example of an irrelevant answer. First, the answer does not deal with either the fatality rate at all. More importantly, though, the discrepancy only arises in country X – so we need something particular to country X that resolves it. (A) ignores country X completely. That can't be right. Some students find answers like (A) attractive sometimes, because it sounds like the statement *could very easily be true*. That is not a consideration here – for this question, we're assuming each of the five answers (in turn) IS true. The right answer isn't the one that sounds like it's the most likely of the five choices to be true – it's the one that would clear up the discrepancy *if it is*.

- (B) Incorrect. This answer choice is much better than (A) – it discusses both country X and the fatality rate. These will be key elements of the right answer. But it doesn't offer us an explanation as to why a higher-than-normal fatality rate occurs in Country X. The information it provides doesn't clear up the confusion caused by the passage. Whether or not most of the fatal cases involve people who don't reside in Country X doesn't help us understand the discrepancy.

(C) Correct. First, we're dealing entirely with Country X, which is a good sign. If the diagnosis only occurs except in the most severe cases, we have an explanation for both facts given in the passage – the mild cases are not diagnosed, which explains the low incidence of Disease P; in other countries, they diagnose those mild cases, resulting in a higher incidence of the disease. However, because only the "most severe cases" are diagnosed, a higher percentage *of people diagnosed* will die from Disease P. The mild cases (that people survive) aren't being considered in Country X, because they haven't been diagnosed.

(D) Incorrect. Completely irrelevant. Again, there is nothing here about either country X, or about the fatality rate. Sometimes putting a name to the variables (like 'Disease P') helps to evaluate an answer or a passage. What if you said to someone, "You know what's weird? In New York, almost nobody gets the measles. But 98% of the people who get measles die from it. How do you explain that?" and that person said, "Well, that's because the number of cases of measles in New York fluctuates a lot from year to year." Hopefully you'll agree that such a response would do nothing at all to address your question!

(E) Incorrect. The best of the wrong answers, in my opinion, because it *does* explain a key element of the passage. It tells why the cases that occur in country X are more likely to be fatal than the cases that occur elsewhere. But there are two elements to the discrepancy; (E) doesn't tell us why country X might have the lowest reported incidence of disease P. So it only provides half of an explanation.

Afterthoughts: Before you start looking at (and getting distracted by) the wrong answer choices, you must try to get a clear idea of what the apparent discrepancy is.

6. Forethoughts: A key word that's easy to miss in the prompt is "evidence." <u>Much more typically</u>, the *premises* ("evidence offered in support of the conclusion") are taken as true, and the *reasoning* (the link between the premises and the conclusion) may be suspect. Here, though, we're going to be attacking the claimed factual support for the conclusion, so as we read the passage, it's the premises we're going to focus on. At a first reading (or even a second), it may be hard to see where the premises are vulnerable to attack. When that happens, don't panic; just move on to the answer choices.

(A) Incorrect. This one is irrelevant – the premises are about the <u>affected</u> otters. New information about unaffected otters may provide more evidence for the argument as a whole (the *reasoning*), but it does not call any of the original premises into question – those premises are all about the ones that *were* affected. Additionally, why would the particular species of the sea otters matter?

(B) Correct. Referring back to the passage, we see that it does make a claim about how many otters that were never found (4/5 – "only a fifth…were ever found").

Moreover, the portion of the passage that (B) refers to is a premise; it's not the conclusion – that would be "The effort was not worthwhile." And we know that the correct answer choice is supposed to be undermining a premise. (B) raises a good point: How we can trust the claim that only a fifth of the otters that died immediately were found? 900 dead otters were found, but the only way we could know that 900 was "a fifth" would be if we knew that 3600 *weren't* found[4]. But how can we count the ones that were never found? Good question...Good answer.

(C) Incorrect. Like (A), this one provides additional information that does not undermine the argument's premises. The evidence is all about the number of otters that were affected – How many were counted, and how many survived. Additional information about the otters that *weren't* affected does not challenge the validity of the evidence about the ones that *were* affected.

(D) Incorrect. Another irrelevant option, largely for the same reasons as (C). (D) is even less relevant. The argument is about whether or not it was worthwhile to try to save sea otters, and the premises all pertain to how many otters were found, and how many survived. In evaluating the writer's conclusion that the efforts were not worthwhile, it doesn't matter whether or carp, or squid, or trout were affected – there were no rescue efforts that we know of that involved any of those species. And information about those species certainly doesn't affect the reliability of the evidence about the otters that were studied.

(E) Incorrect. There is nothing in the passage about cost (let alone "cost per otter"), (E) doesn't "seriously call into question" any evidence offered in the passage. It might "seriously call into the question" the *conclusion* of the passage (for instance, if it cost five dollars to save the 222 otters, then most people would probably think it was "worthwhile"). But the question isn't about undermining the *conclusion*; it asks for something that undermines the *evidence* offered in the passage. (E) does not address the evidence at all.

Afterthoughts: While predicting the correct answer is a very useful skill, both for time and accuracy, it is not always easy to do. Don't spend more than about 15 seconds trying to think of what the right answer should look like. Sometimes that inspiration just isn't forthcoming, and you don't want to waste time stuck in a rut – just move to the answer choices and evaluate each in turn. Take the benefits of the "prediction" method when they readily come to you, and move on when they don't.

7. Forethoughts: This is an assumption question, and assumption questions come in two flavors – 'necessary assumption' and 'sufficient assumption' questions. Most of the

---

[4] If math isn't your thing, I sympathize. For the sake of completeness, though – the passage tells us that 900 dead otters were counted, that number represents a fifth of all of the dead ones. 900 is 1/5 of 4500, so according to the passage, there must have been 4500 dead otters. If 900 were found, then 3600 were not found.

time, the best way to distinguish between them is by looking for specific language indicating that you have a necessary assumption question - in this case, the word 'required' in the question lets you know that this is a necessary assumption question. Assumption questions that lack words like 'required' are sufficient assumption questions[5]. The difference is an important one, because the key technique to use on necessary assumption questions – negation – won't work on sufficient assumption questions. Here's how negation works: For each answer choice, ask yourself, "What if this *weren't* true?" Negating the right answer choice will destroy the argument; if it's a wrong answer choice, the conclusion won't be undermined at all. The negation technique, though, can be time consuming and sometimes confusing to apply to every answer choice, so my preference is to use it to confirm a right answer, or separate two answer choices after eliminating the others.

To narrow down the field of potential answer choices in an assumption question, I look for the place in the argument where the reasoning "jumps the track." Usually, it's in the conclusion, but sometimes, it's between two premises. What happens is, the passage goes from talking about one thing to talking about something else. The missing assumption is a bridge between either two premises, or between a premise and the conclusion.

Here, the "So" not only indicates the conclusion of the passage, it also suggests that the therapeutic value referenced in the second sentence is connected to the first sentence, which must mean it's about the vulnerability to cancer. The final premise in the passage *sequentially* ("as it is clear that...") is the first premise, *conceptually*. It should link to the first sentence in the passage, which in turn likes to the conclusion. However, this last premise doesn't connect support groups to the *immune system*; it connects them to *stress levels*. This is the "broken chain" – we go from a premise about stress levels to one about the immune system. The missing link, or assumption, should connect those two. Here's what the argument looks like, rearranged to close with the conclusion:

Premise: Support Groups → Lower Stress

Premise: Immune system → (connected to) Cancer

Conclusion: Support Groups → (reduce) Cancer ("therapeutic value").

---

[5] The exception is a question that flat-out tells you that something IS assumed by the argument, such as: "Which of the following is an assumption made by the argument?" That's an example of necessary assumption wording too, but it's far less common. Sufficient assumption questions typically say things like, "The conclusion would follow logically if which one of the following is assumed?" You always get that "if" in there. The assumption doesn't HAVE to be made, but if it is, the conclusion follows. So, in a nutshell, in a *sufficient* assumption question, if the (correct answer) assumption is made, the conclusion (which you have to find in the passage) works; in a *necessary* assumption question, if the assumption *isn't* made, then the conclusion *doesn't* work.

The conclusion starts with support groups, and that's covered in the passage ("such groups reduce...stress"). The conclusion ends with "therapeutic value," and that's covered in the passage, too ("vulnerability to cancer"). What's not covered in the passage is how we got from the first premise to the second. We jumped from "reduced stress" to "a better immune system." The assumption will have to cover that leap.

(A) Incorrect. The first sign that should warn you off of this answer is the reference to "learning to function well." That's a phrase that doesn't appear in the passage, which means that functioning well is not tied into anything else in the argument, and therefore is probably not a component of a necessary assumption. If you were to apply the negation technique to this answer choice – if patients could *not* learn to function well – the argument would not become fatally flawed. The conclusion does not depend on their functioning well; it depends on their immune systems and whether or not they're weakened.

(B) Incorrect. This answer may sound pretty good. The psychologist *does* disagree with those who believe that disease "is a purely biochemical phenomenon." However, his position doesn't require reject that it's a biochemical phenomenon "at all." He simply believes that something that *isn't* biochemical (support groups) may affect processes that *are*. The argument survives the negation technique. If we said that disease is (at least) a partly biochemical process, that doesn't destroy the conclusion that support groups can help.

(C) Correct. This is what we're looking for – a connection between stress and the immune system. The psychologist says that support groups help. How? They reduce the patient's stress levels (stated premise); without that reduction there's a greater chance the patient's immune system will be weakened (assumption in choice (C)); the weakened immune system would increase their vulnerability to cancer (stated premise). So we have a viable connection between the support group and the vulnerability to cancer – *but only if we accept choice (C)* – the connection between the other two premises.

Look what happens if we apply the negation technique – assume that (C) is false, i.e. assume that stress does not weaken the immune system. Now, the conclusion – that support groups have therapeutic value – is destroyed. Support groups reduce stress (premise), but that's as far as the argument gets. If we assume that stress does nothing to the immune system, then reducing stress doesn't matter to anything else in the argument. The premise connecting a weakened immune system to cancer wouldn't matter, because there would be no connection between stress and a weakened immune system. We'd be left with two unconnected assertions – support groups lower stress; and a weakened immune system makes you more likely to get cancer – and no basis for the conclusion that connects the support groups, from the first statement, to the cancer vulnerability, from the second.

- (D) Incorrect. This is another answer choice that is attractive at first glance. It seems consistent with the psychologist's point, and it probably is. There are a couple of big problems with it, though. First, it's essentially just a restatement of a stated premise – "participation in such groups reduces participants' stress levels." Assumptions are *unspoken* premises that the speaker left out of the argument. Second, the psychologist is talking about *reducing* stress levels; (D) has a typical flaw – it overstates the case by referring to *eliminating* the stress. Completely eliminating stress isn't *necessary* to that conclusion. For example, if stress were reduced by 50%, that would presumably have therapeutic value; eliminating stress altogether is not required.

- (E) Incorrect. This has the right elements (the stress / immune system link), and if you're looking for that link, you might mistakenly grab this choice. The problem is, it confuses cause and effect (a common, heavily tested error). The psychologist believes that by reducing your stress, you can cause a beneficial change in your immune system – in other words, stress level is the cause and the immune system is the effect. This answer choice gets it backward, by saying that stress is a "symptom" of a weakened immune system – in other words, the immune system is the cause, and the stress is the effect.

Afterthoughts: Although a couple of the answer choices may have content that seems reasonable, if you focus on linking the key terms involved in the passage's leap – stress and the immune system – you should be able to narrow your choices down to C and E. Then it's a question of realizing the key difference between those two – whether stress is the cause and the change in the immune system is the effect, or vice-versa.

Again, the argument, with the assumption included, is very straightforward:

Support groups → Lower stress. (last premise)

Lower stress → Healthier immune system. (assumption (answer choice (C))

Healthier immune system → Less vulnerability to cancer. (first premise)

Therefore: Participating in support groups has therapeutic value (conclusion, 'therapeutic' meaning 'assists in the cure').

The arrows are directional, though; they signify one way streets. We need to get *from* the stress *to* the healthier immune system, because "stress" comes from a premise.

8. Forethoughts: This is a "find the conclusion" type of question, and the conclusion will be explicitly stated – the conclusion was "drawn." In contrast, other questions may say

things like, "The statements above *would* most strongly support which of the following," in which case we won't find the conclusion in the passage. Here, the main conclusion is the statement that the other elements of the passage all work to support. That certainly seems to be the first sentence.

- (A) Incorrect. This sounds ok at first glance – the main idea of the paragraph seems to be about the benefits of adobe in certain environments. One problem, though, is that the passage identifies adobe as "ideal," not merely "a suitable substitute." Another problem is that passage only recommends adobe for the desert in particular, not everywhere that heat-conduction properties are important. Adobe conducts heat "very slowly"; maybe in an environment *other than the desert*, it might be important to conduct heat quickly. Remember, we're not being asked to decide whether or not (A) is true; just if it's the main conclusion of the passage. It's not; the passage is only about the desert, and whether adobe is "ideal."

- (B) Incorrect. This statement about the properties of adobe buildings in the desert is being used to support a further point – that it's "ideal." The statement in (B) is arguably a conclusion, because it's based on the statement that adobe conducts heat slowly (another clue is the conclusion-indicating phrase "as a result"), but whether you construe it as a premise or a conclusion, it's not the <u>main</u> conclusion; it advances the argument even further. (See the Afterthoughts for an explanation of an "intermediate conclusion").

- (C) Incorrect. Similar to (B). Again, the daytime and nighttime temperatures of adobe are furthering the conclusion that adobe is "ideal" (in the desert). Also, to me, the passage implies (gradual) temperature changes in adobe houses, i.e. the temperature doesn't seem to be "constant" – the passage tells us that they're cool during the day and warm at night (though those could be terms referring to the same temperature, i.e. 75 degrees is "cool" during the day and "warm" at night).

- (D) Incorrect. This answer choice also contains the word "constant." If "constancy" were the main conclusion, though, it would appear in the passage. But there's a glaring omissions here. Yes, the passage states that a material that enables houses to maintain pleasant (if not constant) temperatures is ideal – but the main conclusion of the passage is that *adobe* is that material. The main point of the passage is about adobe's usefulness as a building material; everything else supports that notion. So an answer choice that doesn't mention adobe at all is not going to be the correct answer, even if that answer choice is accurate. Remember, it's not enough for a Logical Reasoning answer to be *true*; it also has to answer the question asked.

- (E) Finally…simple and direct. The only change from the passage is that "ideal" became "especially suitable." Sounds synonymous to me. This is exactly what the passage is trying to demonstrate, with everything else in the passage acting in support.

Afterthoughts: This question type shouldn't be that tough when you get used to it. The first key is to identify the main conclusion of the passage, and the second key is to make sure that nothing critical got "mistranslated" on the way to the answer choice.

9. Forethoughts: Another "discrepancy" question (compare #5). This time, the apparent discrepancy is pretty straightforward – The first study found a lot more patterned stems than the second study, even though they were done in the same geographical area. So I need an answer choice that distinguishes between the two studies in such a way that a higher percentage of patterned stems is found the first time. The question seems too broad to suggest a predicted answer; we'll just have to see what the answer choices look like.

> (A) Incorrect. This might be superficially attractive. More plants in the first study might mean more patterned stems; the problem is, the study found more patterned stems *on a percentage basis*. The examiners do this quite a bit – whenever a question is at all mathematical – about anything that can be quantified – there will be wrong answer choices that change the point of reference of what's being measured. This is a classic example: The passage talks about the *percentage* of patterned stems. The *total number* of plants studied is irrelevant. (A) might explain it if they found <u>more plants</u> the first time, but it does nothing to explain why a higher percentage had patterned stems.
>
> (B) Incorrect. A classic distraction-type answer choice. We want an answer to the question, "Why were there more patterned stems for Species X in the first study than the second study?" Saying that information was also collected about Species Y and Z does absolutely nothing to answer that question.
>
> (C) Incorrect. This is (A) all over again – a disparity in the number of plants studied, whether it's expressed directly, as here, or described as "most populous," as in (A), is a completely different issue than the *percentage* of patterned vs. non-patterned stems. Irrelevant to the question asked.
>
> (D) Correct. This choice distinguishes between the studies, and it does so in such a way that it resolves our discrepancy. A "broader"[6] definition of patterned means that more stems would fall under that definition. In other words, even if the stems from the first study were identical to the stems in the second study (as we would expect, since we're talking about the same plant species in the same

---

[6] Unfortunately, there's always some vocabulary testing going on in the LSAT. "Broader" here simply means more inclusive. If that's a definition you're not familiar with, it's going to be hard to work this one out.

geographical area), some would be called "patterned" in the first study but not the second, because the second would use a narrower definition.

- (E) Incorrect. Similar to (B), an irrelevant distraction. Observations were made about whether the stems were patterned in both studies; whether that information is the study's primary goal or secondary goal doesn't explain why there was a greater percentage of patterned stems in the second study.

Afterthoughts: The correct answer here illustrates a common way in which arguments may be flawed, often dismissed as "semantics." A mathematical property states that if A=B and A=C, then B=C. The problem is when the first 'A' doesn't mean what the second 'A' means. If "patterned" means one thing as applied to group B, and another thing as applied to group C, then there will be differences between B and C.

10. Forethoughts: In a flaw question, I'm always going to try to predict the right answer up front. The writer claims that the petition supports his position that the editor's approach would harm the fishing. But the petition just says that they prefer pits in another area. There's nothing about the letter writers that says why they oppose the editor; the writer just assumed that they object for the same reason he does. Maybe they think the proposed location is wrong for some reason totally unrelated to fishing. They signed, but that doesn't tell us *why* they signed.

- (A) Incorrect. There's one huge problem with this answer choice: We aren't even told what the editor's preferred approach is! We have no idea whether or not the letter writer is accurately representing it. Since we don't know what the editor's view is, we have no evidence that it's being "distorted."

- (B) Incorrect. This is certainly a true statement – there's no evidence establishing the viability of the sand-capped pits. The problem is, the letter's conclusion is that *the editor's approach would damage commercial fishing operations*; whether or not the sand-capped pits alternative is "viable" has no bearing on this. Even if the alternative isn't viable, if the editor's approach would damage commercial fishing operations, the letter's conclusion is correct.

- (C) Incorrect. This is just a poor answer choice. Bias certainly exists in some cases, and it certainly undermines arguments (as you'll find out in your Evidence classes and when you start impeaching witnesses as an attorney), but there is no evidence of it in the passage. If we're going to "accurately describe a reasoning flaw," then we have to observe that the flaw exists in the passage; we can't pick a random reasoning flaw.

- (D) Correct. This does not match the predicted answer, but it is pretty good. The only evidence offered by the letter writer is the petition. The claim that the editor's approach would harm commercial fishing is an assertion. The "evidence" is that 20,000 people agree with the letter writer. Again, looking ahead to your Evidence classes and the practice of law, when it comes to opinion evidence, ideally, it's *expert* opinion we're looking for. In fact, attorneys spend a great deal of time at trial establishing expertise through BTE (Background, Training, and Experience) so that juries will respect their opinions. As for the 20,000 people who signed the petition, we have no evidence that their opinions should be given any weight at all. Because this choice doesn't match the predicted answer, I would mark it as one to get back to, then scope out (E).

(E) Incorrect. There is nothing in the passage about whether or not a "third option" exists that would satisfy all the interested parties, and the letter writer doesn't seem to care about that, anyway. His concern is the viability of commercial fishing in the area – not keeping "all the interested parties" happy. This is a typical irrelevant answer choice. Notice that the letter writer is not explicitly advocating the *second* option (the sand-capped pits); the fact that 20,000 *other* people prefer the bits is just being used as evidence that the editor's option is bad. This answer choice *could* be good if the passage had another conclusion; for instance, if the conclusion was that because the editor's option would damage commercial fishing operations, therefore, the sand-capped pits must be used. Then he could be criticized as overlooking the possibility that there were other options. Again, though, the conclusion of the passage is that one specific option (the editor's) would damage commercial fishing operations. Flaws, assumptions, strengthen/weaken questions, etc. all must be evaluated in terms of the conclusion. That's why you have to identify the conclusion when you read an argument in the Logical Reasoning sections. That's the key part of the passage.

Afterthoughts: In addition to the flaw that the examiners were looking for – that the 20,000 petition-signers don't have any known qualifications – there's actually a second flaw with the passage: Just because 20,000 people prefer the sand-capped pits alternative doesn't mean that the editor's approach would damage commercial fishing operations; maybe they have other reasons for favoring the sand-capped pits. This was the flaw I was looking for with my predicted answer. I could have just put the correct flaw in the "Forethoughts" section, but I wanted to include my actual thought process the first time I read this question, because I think it illustrates an important point – you have to be able to think on your feet when you come up with a predicted answer and it doesn't appear as part of one of the five alternatives. Predicting answer choices is a *very* useful technique, but it's not foolproof. Sometimes, the answer you've predicted isn't listed as one of your options. Don't panic. Accept that your prediction was off, and *get over it*. The answer that will be credited isn't your prediction – it's one of the five choices that are listed. So get busy evaluating the actual options. They don't take write-in votes on the LSAT.

This question also illustrates the importance of identifying the conclusion in a passage – underline it, draw stars, put it in brackets...whatever works for you. The evidence here is that 20,000 people prefer a different approach than the editor; the conclusion is that the editor's approach would damage commercial fishing operations. That's a pretty big leap, and it's a lot easier to see the problem with it if you've identified the difference between the premises and the conclusion, rather than just looking at the passage as a general collection of sentences. Not all sentences in the passage are created equal; the conclusion is the most important part of the argument.

11. Forethoughts: Remember question 1: "Y is true because of X." The speaker claims to have the reason(s) that something is true. The argument is strengthened by one of two things: either the connection between X and Y gets stronger, or an alternative explanation gets weaker. Here, for instance, my restatement (to myself) is something like: "Most universities offer a more cosmopolitan education today because of more diverse history textbooks." The "because of" is a little misleading in that restatement – the speaker isn't saying that the textbooks are *causing* the difference in the educations offered; he's saying that the textbooks demonstrate that the conclusion is true. I don't need to identify a cause/effect relationship, though; I'm just trying to make sure I have a clear idea of what main premise and conclusion the passage is trying to tie together.

- (A) Incorrect. This answer choice includes one of the key terms – the history courses (the history textbooks are connected to the history courses) – but it doesn't do anything to connect the courses to the quality of education. The conclusion is about what the universities *offer*, not what interests the students. (A) doesn't give us any evidence that the universities are responding to the student interest, for instance, by offering *more* of those "comprehensive" classes.

- (B) Incorrect. This could be superficially attractive, because "innovative study-abroad programs" might be considered an indication of an in-depth, cosmopolitan education. But the fact that "many" students at some universities participate in such programs doesn't mean that most universities offer more such educations than "ever before." We can't go from "many," which is vague, to "most" which specifically means "more than half." We also don't have a basis here for the "ever before" line, because we don't know how many people were participating in such programs in the past. The inclusive textbooks are new (from the passage), but maybe many students in the older classes using the older textbooks participated in these programs, too. The passage doesn't isolate the important basis for comparison.

- (C) Correct. Here we have the relevant comparison that's missing from (B). The textbooks connect directly to the cosmopolitan education (Remember, for each answer choice, we assume that it's true; so for (C), we have the connection between the passage's conclusion and main premise as discussed in the forethoughts). Also, we have the "more than ever before" comparison, because these inclusive textbooks were not required before. So there wasn't much of a cosmopolitan education before (because the textbooks, which were not in use, reflect the cosmopolitan education), but now there is.

- (D) This answer choice *weakens* the conclusion. Again, the speaker's position is that inclusive history classes = cosmopolitan education. If this answer choice were true, though, it would seem that inclusiveness in the history department doesn't mean inclusiveness in general – this should lead us to believe that we *can't* generalize from the history classes to students' educations in general.

- (E) This one is pretty bland, largely because of the word "alone," which qualifies (limits) the answer choice too much for it to be useful. Moreover, if students don't get cosmopolitan educations from history courses *alone*, that still leaves open the possibility that they might get them from other courses. If *that's* true, then the passage really says nothing, because the students of the past, despite not getting an in-depth, cosmopolitan education from those history courses, might have gotten one from other sources (and the suggestion of the passage is that they didn't, at least in comparison to today's students).

Afterthoughts: This one is on the confusing side. Maybe the best way to keep it straight is to think of things in their most basic terms – What are the things being connected? How strong is the connection? Here, it's diversity in history courses being connected to a cosmopolitan education. From the passage, we don't know how strong the connection is; it's sort of a blanket assertion. Here, the "Strengthen the Argument" correct answer is the one that fleshes out that connection and makes it a little more reliable.

12. Forethoughts: As always, I want to predict the answer before looking at the options, if possible. Here, though, I think it's difficult (but more power to you if you were able to zero on in on the correct answer before seeing the choices). I find it murky enough that I would just move onto the answer choices.

- (A) Correct. Maybe at the first read, you wouldn't latch onto it as the clear-cut right answer, but it should at least sound pretty good and be marked as one to get back to if nothing better comes along. It meets the important criteria – 1) it's *true* that the argument fails to consider that incomplete reports may still contain important information, and 2) it also illustrates a flaw in the argument. If you marked the argument's conclusion "such disclosure actually undermines the governement's goal…" this will be easier to see; the conclusion is that because the reports won't be *complete*, they won't be *informative*. (A) points out that this is a false dichotomy; even incomplete reports can inform the public.[7]

(B) Incorrect. Beware, Beware, Beware irrelevant answer choices like this – the question is about whether an action that was taken will undermine a stated goal – making the public "more informed." It is *entirely* irrelevant whether anyone has the "right" to the information. Similar answer choices might discuss the government's "motive" for taking a particular action, or whether something "should" have been done. We're concerned here with the "what," not the "why." The only thing we care about is the link between disclosing the reports and informing the public – Do they make the public more informed, or not?

(C) Incorrect. This is a good example of a common wrong answer type, and it's an attractive one. The idea that there aren't other sources of information absolutely *does* tie into the argument, because the passage connects "airlines will be much less likely..." to "undermines...making the public more informed." BUT saying that the argument presumes that it is "impossible" to get the information any other way overstates the case. Always take a hard look at answer choices that use terms like "never," "always," "invariably," etc. The conclusion is only that the goal is "undermined." If the information is hard to get, that could undermine the goal of making the public more informed; the argument doesn't require that finding the information be "impossible."

(D) Check out the discussion of B, above – again, the issue is what *will* happen, not who *should* be held responsible for the reporting. Regardless of why the policy was adopted, the argument in the passage is only concerned with its consequences. I call this wrong answer type the "moral" answer. If the passage is about what will or won't happen, avoid answer choices that deal with things like "why" it might happen, what "should" happen, what someone "motives" are, etc.

Note that *in some circumstances*, a "moral answer" <u>could</u> be right, but it would have to match up to the argument in the passage. For instance, if a passage is, "Public officials should not raise taxes unless a deficit exceeds 10% of the budget," then a conclusion about what the officials "should" do could be justified.

(E) This may very well be true (nothing in the passage tells us that the writer considered whether the publication will have an effect on the airlines' revenues), but it is also completely irrelevant to the argument. Whether or not it affects their revenue doesn't necessarily affect the goal of making the public more

---

[7] Notice that the conclusion is about whether the public will be "more" informed (as opposed to, say, "fully" informed). The reports don't necessarily have to be *complete* to make the public "more informed."

informed. Just another reminder that to be a correct answer, it is not enough for a statement to be true – keep in mind the question that's being asked.

Afterthoughts: Not much here in the way of takeaway points. For each answer choice, simply ask yourself first, "Is this statement true?" and second, "Does it matter?"

13. Forethoughts: A "Weaken the Argument" question. These questions are prime candidates for an "alternative explanation" scenario. Again, in simplest terms, the argument can be summarized as "X is true because of Y." So I'm always trying to think of something other than Y (call it Z) that could explain X. If I can think of a "Z", the argument will be weakened if Z is true. Here, it's pretty easy to do – I would state the argument as, "People aren't really as motivated by money as economists think, because surveys do not reflect it." This suggests a great alternative explanation – I'm looking for an answer choice that says something like, "People lie on surveys." Maybe people don't want survey takers to think they're greedy, money-motivated people, for instance.

Unfortunately, there was no such answer choice! I could have led with the line of thought that gets straight to the heart of the answer, but I wanted the "Forethoughts" to reflect my actual thoughts reading the passage for the first time. It's also a more honest look at the process – predicting is a great technique, but it's not 100%. You have to know what to do when it doesn't work – Don't get tied to your prediction; evaluate the answer choices on their own merits.

- (A) Incorrect. This choice is off-point. There's nothing in the passage about "all the goods they desire," and even if this statement were true, how would it weaken the argument? The conclusion is that economists overestimate the influence of money on job choices. (A) doesn't undermine that conclusion. A good test for relevance is to think about the conclusion with the assumption that the given answer choice is false, then also with the assumption that it's true. Here, whether or not I believe that high wages allow people to have all of the goods they desire doesn't change what I think about whether economists overestimate the degree to which money motivates job choices.

- (B) Incorrect. I know my prediction was off (since it wasn't an answer choice), so I don't know exactly what I'm looking for, but this can't be it. *Of course* people would prefer the high wage job if other things were equal; the point of the survey is that they don't necessarily prefer the high wage job when other things *aren't* equal – i.e. when the jobs offer different advantages and disadvantages. Saying that people want the high-paying job when it's the only factor to consider…that doesn't tell us anything.

- (C) Correct. It's an easy answer to pass over, but if we take a careful review of the passage, we may notice (I missed it the first time; did you?) that the economist was talking about "financial rewards," while the surveys talk about "high salary." It's easy to equate the two, but perhaps there are "financial rewards" *other than salary*, like health or retirement benefits. How does this weaken the argument? If the benefits "vary considerably," then the economist AND the survey could both be right – a person could be very interested in a job without a high salary (consistent with the survey) but only if it had high financial (non-salary) benefits (consistent with the economist's position). This weakens the argument, because the argument's claim is that if the survey is accurate, the economist is wrong.

(D) Incorrect. This may be a true statement, but it doesn't weaken the argument. The question is about the economists' position that financial rewards provide *the strongest incentive* to choose one job over another. The speaker argues that in light of the survey, the economist is wrong. Whether or not people enjoy challenges and difficult jobs is an entirely separate question. Or look at it this way: Since the conclusion is that the economists are *wrong*; the right answer should suggest that the economists could be *right* – financial rewards really *are* the number 1 factor in choosing a job. Let's say that (D) is true (the question asks us to evaluate each answer choice on the assumption that it's true), and people DO enjoy job challenges, if their efforts are rewarded. How would that make it more likely that the economists are right? There's just no connection there.

(E) Incorrect. This should be easy to dismiss. It's important to remember that you shouldn't dismiss this choice because it sounds like it's not true (as this one does, to me); the question requires that you assume that it IS true. So, again (as with (D)), let's say that some people really *don't* know that jobs with high salaries leave no time for recreation. Does that really hurt the argument about whether or not the economists are wrong? Remember, the entire argument is that the survey shows that the economists are wrong – completely unrelated.

Afterthoughts: First and foremost, remember...make a prediction, but if you don't see it among the answer choices – move on! Second, a lot of wrong answer choices may be true statements, but they're still wrong answers. In fact, very often (as here), you're supposed to assume that they're all true, anyway. I see a lot of students get these questions wrong by selecting the answer choice that sounds most likely to be true. That's the incorrect approach. The question to ask is, how does each answer choice relate to the argument (especially the conclusion)? Finally, try to be aware of the subtle shifts in an argument – when it goes from talking about one thing to talking about something else. Here, the switch from "financial rewards" to "high salary." The exact words don't have to be identical, but if they're not at least synonymous, the answer may very well hinge on the difference – as it does here.

14. Forethoughts: Any time there's an assumption question, I'm on the lookout for terms that show up in the conclusion out of nowhere. Here, the students' average grades make an appearance in the very last line, tied to absolutely nothing. *Huge* red flag. It's a long passage, but successfully untangling it will make finding the right answer a breeze. The Editorial disagrees with the parents, whose ultimate conclusion was that small class size leads to more *student engagement*. In other words, the conclusion is that small class size would NOT lead to more student engagement. The reason is that studies found that small class sizes had no effect on *grades*. So the editorial is implying some sort of relationship between "grades" and "student engagement" (or possibly one of the other facets of small class size). I'm looking for an answer choice that connects those two terms. The right answer almost has to reference grades – *the unchanged grades are the only evidence cited in support of the conclusion*. I also note that this is a <u>necessary</u> assumption question; the tip-off is the word "required" in the prompt. Therefore, I can use the 'negation' technique to verify my answer (see Question #7 in this section).

- (A) Incorrect. This choice doesn't reference the grades all, so it's hard to see how it's going to work. Moreover, it refers to the size of the *schools* ("large"), which doesn't necessarily have anything to do with the size of the *classrooms* (but might trap someone in a hurry). All in all, though, an irrelevant choice.

- (B) Incorrect. A superficially attractive choice that is actually irrelevant. First, again, it ignores the grades. There's a more important problem, though. The argument focuses on what happens when the teachers have more time for each student. In other words, the relevant comparison is between Student A if he got, say, 20 minutes of teacher time vs. Student A if he got, say, 40 minutes of teacher time (because class sizes were reduced). This answer, though, instead compares Student A to Student B (by saying that they get the same amount of time, regardless of whether it's 20 minutes, or 40 minutes, or any other amount). It doesn't matter that each student gets the *same* amount of individualized attention as each other student; the question is, would it be better if they got MORE? Answer B does not address that question at all.

- (C) Incorrect. The Editorial is not making this assumption, and does not need to. In fact, it's probably assuming the opposite. Let's say there are 30 students in each class currently. If the law requires a limit of 20 students per class, then the schools would presumably hire MORE teachers[8]. Regardless, (C) is beside the point. The question is about what would happen if class sizes were smaller; what steps might have to be taken to bring about those smaller classes (e.g. hiring or firing teachers) is a separate issue. Here's an obscure analogy: If my argument is

---

[8] Example: Say you have 100 students in a school, in 4 classes (25 students per class). If you require a maximum of 20 students per class, you have to now put those 100 students into 5 classes, so you need another teacher.

that tacos would be better than spaghetti for dinner, that doesn't depend on the assumption that having tacos would require buying tortillas.

(D) Correct. The only answer choice that involves grades, so I like it already. The researchers say that because the students' average grades haven't changed, then the students are not more engaged. Or, contrapositively, if the students were more engaged, then their average grades would reflect that change. This connection between two variables is the very definition of a "correlation," so this answer choice is 100% on target.

(E) Incorrect. Parental support for the proposal is completely irrelevant. Again, the issue is what will happen if the proposal is adopted. This is a common type of wrong answer choice. If fact, we just saw it; it's the "moral answer" choice from question 12. The parents' reason(s) just don't matter to the conclusion.

Afterthoughts: If you liked one of the irrelevant choices here, reread the passage and think about the Editorial's point. The wrong answer choices don't address that point. Also, remember the negation test: If (D) were not true – in other words, if there were no correlation between grades and student engagement – then the researchers' argument falls apart. They concluded that because the grades did not go up, they were no more engaged. If there were no correlation between student engagement and grades, there would be no basis for that conclusion. That's the key to a "necessary assumption" question. The right answer is the choice that the argument can't survive without.

15. Forethoughts: Reading over the passage in search of a prediction, I notice that while Camille claims that the *amount* of savings is exaggerated, Rebecca says that she has saved money, but ignores the question of the amount of the savings. That discrepancy grabs my attention, and I'll be expecting an answer choice that addresses it. Also, I read the question first, so I was forewarned that as I read the passage, I needed to look for a problem with Rebecca's reasoning, that helped focus my attention.

(A) Incorrect. The installation cost will certainly bear on the amount of the total savings, but the argument seems to be about how much can be saved on the bills – Camille compares volume of water per time unit to the increased time that the water runs – not the total cost/benefit. It seems like both speakers are assuming that the cost of installation is less than the savings; even Camille, who thinks that the claims of the manufacturers are exaggerated, isn't saying that the faucets don't save *any* money. But there's no reason to think that this assumption is questionable, and it's a separate issue than the argument as to whether or not the manufacturers' claims are exaggerated.

(B) Correct. This is on point, and it's what I was looking for. Rebecca says that because she's saved money, the manufacturer's claims aren't exaggerated, but the question isn't just about the fact that she saved money; it's about whether she saved *as much money* as the manufacturer said she would (if not, the claims ARE exaggerated, even though she saved money). Rebecca's logic is bad because she didn't address that distinction at all, and that's what (B) gets at.

(C) Incorrect. The claims don't all have to be consistent to conclude (as Rebecca does) that their claims are not exaggerated. Let's say that some of them say you can save 5%, and others claim that you can save 10%. Those claims are not consistent, but as long as you save at least 10%, the conclusion that the claims are not exaggerated is fine (or, on the other hand, if you don't save 5%, then the claims *are* all exaggerated, even though they're inconsistent). We have no reason to think that Rebecca is assuming that they're consistent, and for the purposes of the argument, it's not necessary that they be.

(D) Incorrect. Check out the wrong answers in #12, above; this is another "moral" answer. The claims are very clear; do they exaggerate the savings or not? Customer satisfaction is irrelevant. Moreover, we have no reason that I can see to reach *any* conclusion about what Rebecca thinks of other customers' satisfaction.

(E) Incorrect. We don't know what Rebecca thinks would happen if she installed more of these faucets, so it's hard to say that she's taking it for granted. Even if she *were* taking it for granted, why would that be a flaw? It's probably true – if the faucets save money, then more of them might very well save more money. At any rate, what would or wouldn't happen with "more" faucets does not address a position about whether or not the claims are exaggerated.

Afterthoughts: This is a great question for emphasizing the importance of the prediction technique, mostly because (A) is kind of an attractive wrong answer – in my view, the "best" wrong answer we've seen in a while. But if you notice the error that Rebecca made in the passage – going from "any" savings to concluding that the *amount* of savings was exaggerated – then you're much less likely to be distracted by (A). In effect, you're giving yourself a chance to work out the right answer to the question before being biased by the answer choices. Plus, it's really good practice to think about the question without rushing to the answer choices until you've taken a little while to see what you can come up with. Again, though, don't get carried away; if nothing is hitting you after 15 seconds or so, don't burn up all your time waiting for inspiration.

This is also a good question to illustrate another of my favorite techniques – restating the argument in one simple sentence: X is true, because Y. Rebecca's argument is "The manufacturers' claims are not exaggerated, because my water bills are lower." Put that simply, you should see the problem. If the manufacturers' claims were that she'd save 50%, then it doesn't matter if her bills are 10% lower – the claims are still exaggerated. The only evidence we know she's relying on – lower water bills – is not enough to reach the conclusion that the claims aren't exaggerated, because we have no idea what the claims were or how much she actually saved.

16. Forethoughts: You can pretty much bet that any time an LSAT question involves numbers, or anything that can be quantified at all, they're going to shift the reference point on you. By that I mean they'll try to compare apples to oranges. For instance, the passage might talk about the *number* of people who do something, and there will be wrong answers that talk about the *percentage* of people who do something. Or the premises will talk about the *percentage* of blood in someone's system, and the (flawed) conclusion will talk about the *amount* of alcohol in his system. Always scrutinize the numbers carefully and make sure you understand exactly what they mean. That's usually the key.

Here, the cars count for a lot more of the pollution than the plants. One problem, though, is that they don't really tell us how much of that 30% we can expect to reduce by buying back cars (they also don't tell us how much of the 4% we can fix by remodeling the plants). In other words, the trick here looks like it will involve a shift that the spokesperson has already made: The data are about the percentages of the *problem* (how much of the local air pollution), but the conclusion is about the percentage of the *solution* (how much of it they can fix). Those two things probably aren't the same. I mean, if you could get rid of ALL of the 30% by buying up cars, then the spokesman would be right – that would clearly be best. But what if the program doesn't bring in any cars at all, because owners of old cars like to keep them as classic collectors' items? Then that 30% is still going to be out there.

- (A) Incorrect. Cute, but irrelevant, and a great example of a shift in reference. It doesn't matter what the percentage of the *cars* in the area is. If those 1% of the cars make up 30% of the *pollution*, then buying them back will help a lot. In fact, this would probably be great news for the Spokesperson's proposal, because the company wouldn't have to buy up than many cars to make a big difference.

- (B) Incorrect. Classic irrelevant answer. The conclusion is about *which option would reduce air pollution more.* Whether one option would cost the company money or save the company money has nothing to do with that. This illustrates the importance of clearly identifying the conclusion. For instance, if the spokesperson recited all of the data in the passage, and then his conclusion was, "Clearly, we should remodel the plants," THEN (B) would be relevant – relevant to the question of *what the company should do.* But the passage's actual conclusion (starting with "Clearly…") has nothing to do with what the company "should" do – it's only about which proposal would reduce air pollution more.

- (C) Correct, and possibly easy to overlook. If the buyback program only succeeds in buying back cars that aren't running anyway, then it's not going to do much to clean up that 30%. It's only the old cars *that are still running* that contribute to the 30%. The company could buy back all the broken cars in America and not make any difference at all. That weakens the conclusion, because the small difference that could be made by remodeling the plants would still be better than nothing. This fits the Forethoughts – The old cars are a much larger part of the *problem*, but that doesn't mean they'll be the biggest part of the *solution*.

(D) Incorrect. Another classic irrelevant answer. The conclusion is about <u>which of two specific options</u> – buying old cars or remodeling the factories – will produce a better result; the spokesperson's conclusion is that buying the old cars will. Whether or not there's a third option that's better than either of the other two options (like buying back *newer* cars rather than old ones) is irrelevant to the question of which will have a better impact between the two we're considering.

(E) Incorrect. Again, irrelevant, on so many levels. The citizens might just be happy that the company is doing something. Or maybe it's a sign that pollution is decreasing as a result of the car-buying campaign; that still doesn't tell us whether or not remodeling the factories would have decreased pollution *more*.

Afterthoughts: Always keep that conclusion in mind. Even when it's not a "Find the conclusion" question, it's still critical to understanding the argument and making sure the answer choices address the question that is being asked. And remember – if the conclusion is "Option A is better than Option B," then it won't be weakened OR strengthened by an answer choice that tells you how good (or bad) Option C is.

17. Forethoughts: These types of questions[9] can be confusing, to say the least. All you can really do is try to unravel the passage and the answer choices, and simplify them by stating them in simplest terms. Here's how I'd restate this passage: If humans weren't motivated to sacrifice, then we wouldn't have survived. It can be helpful to do some kind of diagramming for a question like this. That should look something like this:

~~Sacrifice~~ → ~~Survive~~.   (the strikethrough = 'not')

Contrapositive – Humankind survived, so there was sacrifice:

Ancestors survived → Ancestors sacrificed.

Beginning of second sentence:

Sacrifice = (partly) altruism.

Conclusion (second part of second sentence):

---

[9] This is called a "parallel reasoning" question, which is extremely similar to the "parallel flaw" question; you're looking for a pattern of argumentation and applying it to a new context.

Therefore, ancestors = (partly) altruistic.

Now, hopefully, I'm either going to find an answer choice that looks a lot like that breakdown, or four answer choices that look nothing like it.

(A) Correct. ~~Increased Study~~ → ~~Raised Grades~~.

   Contrapositive – Some students have raised their grades, so some students have increased their study:

   Some students raised grades → Some students increased study time.

   Increased Study = Good Time Management.

   Therefore, Some Students = Manage Time Well.

   If you go over this breakdown, piece by piece, you'll see how it maps out and corresponds to the passage, step by step. "Survival" = "Raised grades," and so on. The other answer choices don't correspond like this.

(B) Incorrect. This one breaks down at step one; instead of using the contrapositive, it relies on faulty logic – the inverse: If they don't consume organisms, they can make their own carbohydrate supply; that does *not* mean that if they DO consume insects (other organisms), then they CAN'T make their own carbohydrate supply. Moreover, the first inference was only the starting point in the passage; here, after reaching a (mistaken) conclusion, the argument stops abruptly. From an original conditional statement "If P, then Q," the inverse, which does NOT logically follow, is "If not P, then not Q."

   Here's an example showing why the inverse is not valid: The statement, "If Spot is a dog, then Spot is a mammal" is true, but that doesn't mean that: "If Spot is not a dog, then Spot is not a mammal" is necessarily true. Maybe Spot is a cat.

(C) Incorrect. This one doesn't even get to a conclusion. ~~Protected By Government~~ → ~~Survive~~. If this were parallel to the passage, the next step would be to conclude that because some of them have survived, they must have been protected (contrapositive). Instead, (C) simply gives a reason for this assertion, then stops.

(D) Incorrect. This one goes further than the other two, but not in the way that the passage does. ~~Replaced~~ → Depleted. The next step should be that some resources have not been depleted, so we can conclude that they've been replaced by alternate materials. Remember, the initial passage starts with a conditional relationship, then moves directly to the contrapositive[10]. (D), though, then connects replacement to requiring more power, and conclude that they will be depleted. That doesn't follow the reasoning that the passage took.

- (E) Incorrect. Again, no match. ~~Well Designed~~ → ~~Harmonize~~. The next step should be the contrapositive: Some public buildings harmonize well with their surroundings; then we could conclude that some public buildings are well designed. (E) doesn't do that. Also, the passage reaches a definite conclusion; notice that Choice (E) leaves us hanging with a wishy-washy alternative (either/or) conclusion. Not an attractive choice.

Afterthoughts: This is a question that will repay close study, because it requires you to really dig into the structure of the argument in both the passage and the answer choices. This process is useful for many questions and question types. If you're not familiar with the contrapositive, you need to work on that ASAP; it's the single most important concept on the LSAT. From the conditional statement "If P, then Q" the contrapositive is "If not Q, then not P." The contrapositive is VALID (unlike the inverse). To get the contrapositive, you have to both negate both terms, and switch the sufficient ("if") and necessary ("then") terms. (See footnote 10).

18. Forethoughts: Having read the prompt, I'm reading the passage trying to ask myself what the Bus Driver's underlying justification is (and trying to restate it in my own words. Quietly. Don't talk to yourself aloud during the actual LSAT). It seems pretty clear that the bus driver is relying on the principle that if he was following the law and the other driver wasn't, then he shouldn't be reprimanded, even if he could possibly have prevented the accident. So if that principle is valid, his reasoning is justified.

- (A) Incorrect. This is a sneaky and tempting answer choice. Blaming the driver of the other vehicle, who committed a traffic violation, sounds like it's on point, but the law – and the LSAT – is all about the details. The bus driver doesn't claim that the other driver "*is solely responsible* for the accident." Rather, he claims that he *shouldn't be reprimanded*. If this was your answer choice, I can sympathize. And, actually, if the other driver IS solely responsible, then the bus driver's contention that he shouldn't be reprimanded really *is* well-justified; why

---

[10] The contrapositive isn't really an inference; it's just another way of looking at the same thing. For instance, using the "dog" example, the original statement is "If Spot is a dog, then Spot is a mammal." The contrapositive is, "If Spot is not a mammal, then Spot is not a dog." That's clearly true, and means the same thing. That's what the passage does: If they weren't motivated to sacrifice, they wouldn't have survived; if they did survived, they were motivated to sacrifice.

reprimand him if he's not responsible[11]? It's not bad, as wrong answers go; however, another choice is better.

(B) Incorrect. Unlike (A), this isn't really a good answer choice. Always pay special attention to adverbs in the Logical Reasoning section; they can really draw your attention to the most important parts of a passage or an answer choice. That's a tip I've been giving almost as long as I've been tutoring the LSAT, and hopefully some of my students who took LSAT #60 kept it in mind when they got to this question. If they did, they may have paid special attention to the phrase "*completely* the fault of the driver of another vehicle." (adverb emphasized). The police report said that the bus driver didn't violate any traffic regulations, NOT that the accident was completely the other driver's fault.

(C) Incorrect. This is not a good answer choice either. It's irrelevant on its face, because it refers to what happens when a bus driver "causes a collision to occur by violating a traffic regulation." That's not the case here; the bus driver didn't violate any traffic regulations – the garbage truck driver did. Also, notice that trying to apply this principle would rely on an incorrect inference: the inverse – You can't go from: Cause Collision → Reprimand to: ~~Cause Collision → Reprimand~~. We're trying to justify the bus driver's argument, which has to lead to the conclusion that he *should not* be reprimanded; a principle that indicates when someone *should* be reprimanded will not support the argument.

(D) Incorrect. This choice fails on a couple of levels. First, we know that the driver "might" have been able to avoid the collision, but we don't know if he "*reasonably* (there's that adverb again) could have expected" to. So, we can't apply this principle to the bus driver's situation at all – we don't know if it fits. Second, the bus driver is relying on his following the traffic regulations, so the right answer should pertain to his following the regulations, not to whether or not he could have avoided the accident. The bus driver himself argues that being able to avoid the accident is not relevant to the conclusion ("...*although* I might have been able to..."). Superficially, (D) seems to share a problem with (C) – the fact that it talks about whether the company "should" (rather than "should not") reprimand its drivers. That's actually not one of the problems with (D), because of the word "only." Saying that they "should reprimand only when they do X" logically means that they SHOULD NOT reprimand when they DON'T do X. More on this in the Afterthoughts.

(E) Correct. This is the one that fits the bus driver's argument 110%. Bus involved in collision – check! Collision didn't result from bus driver's violating a regulation –

---

[11] That question is rhetorical: Reprimand because if he can prevent accidents – even accidents he's not responsible for – then he *should* prevent them.

check! Conclusion: shouldn't reprimand the bus driver – Exactly what the bus driver is hoping for. A perfect match.

Afterthoughts: Pretty straightforward question type. The thing to do is ask yourself what conclusion he's reaching, and what he's relying on. Here, the conclusion is that he shouldn't be reprimanded, and the key fact is that no traffic regulations were broken. Back to (D). The word "only" changes a conditional statement in a very important way. The basic form for a conditional statement is "If P, then Q." But if you see a statement like "*Only* if P, then Q[12]," that's not the same thing. "Only if P, then Q" translates to "If NOT P, then NOT Q." In other words, the "only" invokes the negative.[13] The contrapositive, which is also valid, is "If Q, then P."

Here's an illustration, using content that might make it more understandable. If I say, "A person should be put in jail only when he's committed a crime" I'm not saying, "If a person commits a crime, he should be put in jail." Maybe for some crimes, people shouldn't be put in jail – they should just be fined. What I'm saying is, "If a person does NOT commit a crime, he should NOT be put in jail." This is an *extremely* important point. Understanding the incorrect answer choice (D) is probably a more important takeaway point than understanding the correct answer choice (E). If you're not 100% solid on the discussion about the word 'only,' reread the Afterthoughts, Footnotes 12 and 13, and the explanation of (D) a few times. Few things on the LSAT are as important to understand thoroughly as conditional statements. Make that "nothing."

19. Question #19 was not scored.

20. Forethoughts: Another necessary (because of the word "required" in the prompt) assumption question. So I'm on the lookout for jumps in reasoning, and for key terms that show up for the first time in the conclusion. In question 20, there's a gap, and I know it has to do with "today's generation of TV viewers" – a group that is mentioned in the conclusion, but nowhere to be found in the stated premises.

(A) Incorrect. The conclusion isn't about the amount of *time* people spend watching television; it's about their using their imaginations. Since this is a necessary assumption question, we can test this answer choice by saying, "What if this *isn't* true?" If (A) were the right answer, negating it would destroy the answer choice.

---

[12] "Only if P, then Q" means the same thing as "Q, only if P." The order of the terms isn't the important part; it's their logical relevance. The "sufficient" (if) part can come either before or after the "necessary" (then) part.
[13] This "invokes the negative" idea is very important. Here's another example: "Only if you pass the bar will you be a lawyer" is NOT a statement about what will happen if you pass the bar. Passing the bar doesn't necessarily mean you'll be a lawyer. Maybe you'll pass the bar then go to med school. Or pass the bar then win the Lotto and never work again. It's a statement about what happens if you DON'T pass the bar. If you DON'T pass the bar, you WON'T be a lawyer." The "won't" is implied by the "only."

But it doesn't. Let's say that people used to listen to the radio for 4 hours a day, but now they watch TV for 3 hours a day. That wouldn't hurt the conclusion.

(B) Incorrect. The point of the passage isn't about the "familiarity" of various entertainment media. It's about the fact that with radio, because you can't visualize what's happening, you really have to engage your imagination and think about it. It has nothing to do with familiarity; it's simply a function of the fact that radio is a non-visual medium. Besides, we can't even evaluate this answer choice – The passage doesn't tell us whether TV or radio is more familiar.

(C) Incorrect. This is another of those "moral answers" that are just about always wrong. The conclusion is about whether this generation uses imagination more than previous generations did. Whether or not television is "particularly undesirable" is irrelevant to that question. The Historian *may*, in fact, think that television IS particularly undesirable (or he may not), but the issue here is, would his argument fall apart if it weren't? Definitely not.

(D) Correct. What if this statement weren't true? That would mean that something HAS filled the gap left by radio as a medium for exercising the imagination. In that case, the conclusion that today's viewers don't exercise their imaginations as much would fall apart. If something *does* fill the gap (in exercising our imaginations) left by radio, there's no basis (in the passage) for concluding that today's TV viewers don't do it. This is what the Historian left out of the stated argument – he clearly things that not only does television not provide us a regular opportunity to exercise our imaginations, but *nothing else does, either*.

(E) Incorrect. This is somewhat attractive, but it's not necessary to the Historian's conclusion, for a few reasons. For instance, the "thinking" that radio dramas required is explained as imagination-based – picturing the visual elements they couldn't see – but maybe TV involves thinking that doesn't involve the exercise of imagination, like calculating a math problem. So you can negate this answer choice (negated version: "Television requires its viewers to think about what they see") without killing the conclusion that TV viewers use their imaginations less. That is, today's TV viewers might think about what they're watching on TV, but still use their imaginations less often than radio listeners used to.

Afterthoughts: Remember, the key to a necessary assumption question is, "What would happen to the argument if this answer choice were false?" Compare (C) and (D) again. If (C) were false – if television WERE NOT a "particularly undesirable" form of entertainment, that wouldn't destroy the conclusion that television viewers exercise their imaginations less than radio listeners did. On the other hand, if (D) were false – if something DID fill the gap left by radio for exercising the imagination – then the conclusion would fail – we wouldn't know that people today don't exercise their imaginations as much as they did in the past merely because they don't listen to radio dramas anymore; they might do something else (*other than TV*) that works just as well.

21. Forethoughts: Here, I'm going to have to translate the flaw into another fact pattern (because the subject matter in the answer choices won't match the subject matter of the passage). I have to start by identifying the flaw and articulating it in general terms. There is a fairly long chain of inferences in the passage. Did you see where it broke down? Here's the chain, from beginning to end (premises, then conclusion):

P1: All Candidates → Small Business Owner

P2: Small Business Owner (most) → Competent Manager

P3: All Competent Managers → Have skills for Good Mayor (equivalent of "none lacks")

Conclusion: Candidates (most) → Have skills for Good Mayor

It seems like a good chain, from candidate to small business owner to competent manager to having the skills to be a good mayor. The problem is "most"; just because all candidates are small business owners, that doesn't mean you can go from "most small business owners" (P2) to "most candidates" (conclusion). What if the candidates are from that minority of business owners who AREN'T competent managers? Here's a simplified version of the flaw with familiar people: Let's say Sidney Poitier, Denzel Washington, and Halle Berry are the only candidates running for Mayor of Los Angeles. Here's the passage's flaw, in action: All of the candidates are Oscar winners. Most Oscar winners are Caucasian. Therefore, most of the candidates are Caucasian. Oops! That's what happens when you try to carry a "most" from one category to another. That's what we're looking for from the answer choices.

(A) Incorrect:

Management (most) → Worked Sales Dept.

All Sales Dept → 1 yr Experience

All 1yr Exp → Understands Marketing

Upper Management (most) → Understands marketing.

To evaluate this answer choice, you have to look at the second sentence first; it's really "first" logically (if you look at the conclusion, it's about management, not people who work in sales); to follow the chain logically, you need to arrange it as I have, above. There are two potential problems with this answer, depending on how you interpret one part of it – the switch from "Management" to "Upper Management." It sounds like those are two different things, in which case the entire answer choice just goes out the window – we don't have *any* information specific to "upper management" (this error is not the problem with the main passage).

Alternatively, if you want to take the position that "Management" and "Upper Management" *are* the same thing[14], then there's an entirely different problem with this answer choice – it's not flawed! The chain of "All" from the Sales Department to Understanding Marketing (through the "One Year of Experience" link), means that this is actually a valid argument – if Most Management has worked in the Sales Department, then Most Management DOES understand marketing. Compare the streamlined argument that I've lain out with the arrows for this answer choice to the one in the passage, and you should notice that there's a subtle but important difference between the two, related to how and where the "All" and "Most" categories are set up. If we *start* with the "most," then the passage works fine.

(B) Correct:

All Menu Items → Fat Free

Fat Free Food/Drink (most) → Sugar Free

All Sugar Free → Low Cal

Conc: Menu Items (Most) → Low Cal

Verdict: Correct! See how the "All" and "Most" categories line up with the original passage? This is what we're after. Some Fat Free items may NOT be sugar free, and for all we know, those are the ones on the menu. Just like some Oscar winners may NOT be Caucasian, and those may be the ones running for Mayor. Just like some small business owners may NOT be competent managers.

(C) Incorrect:

Without running through the whole "mapping" process (I've done the first two, plus the passage; your turn), there's a clear problem with this choice at the outset – the *passage's* flaw is a mistaken leap from a "Most" in the passage to "Most" in the conclusion. Here, the conclusion is categorical (referring to "no" books). This answer choice *is* flawed (Do you see why? Hint: Maybe some of Ed's books are among those hardcover books that aren't more than 100 pages long), but that's a side issue, because its flaw isn't the same as the passage's.

---

[14] Not recommended, by the way. The LSAT, like the law itself, thrives on specificity. You should *not* take it upon yourself to equate "management" and "upper management." The analysis is continued, however, to demonstrate that this answer choice would be fatally flawed *even if* they were the same thing.

(D) Incorrect:

>All Festival Films → Under 1 Hour
>
>Under 1 Hour (Most) → Not Commercially Successful
>
>All Under 1 Hour → No Intermission
>
>Conclusion: Festival Films (Most) → No Intermission

>This is a rather unusual answer choice, in that the bit about being commercially successful is a complete red herring! It doesn't lead anywhere. You can delete the second premise, and you're left with a perfectly valid argument – all of the festival films are under an hour, which means it's true...they *don't* have an intermission. The conclusion is actually an understatement – not only do "most" films at the festival lack and intermission; ALL of the films at the festival lack an intermission[15]. Being a valid argument, this answer choice is, of course, *not* parallel to the passage, which is flawed.

(E) Incorrect:

>Bicycle Helmets Sold in Store → Plastic
>
>Bicycle Helmets Sold in Store (most) → Rubber
>
>All Helmets with Rubber → Plastic
>
>Conclusion: Helmets Sold in Store with Plastic (most) → Rubber

>The clear problem with (E) is that the conclusion is about all helmets, not just bicycle helmets. Most of the *bicycle* helmets have rubber in them, but there may be a zillion *non-bicycle* helmets that have plastic but not rubber.

Afterthoughts: This one will repay careful study. It's kind of a pain to navigate, but it's worth reviewing, off the clock. In particular, make sure you understand why the first two premises in choice (A) really had to be thought through in reverse order to make the argument understandable, and also why some of the answer choices aren't (or might not be) actually flawed. It's a tough question to handle under time pressure, but a great one to really dig into for improvement.

22. Forethoughts: The conclusion here is only barely tied to the stated premises. Language is used as a point of reference, but the only real premise about money is that it is a convention that was invented, and the conclusion is that it was invented

---

[15] In casual conversation, when we say "most," we imply "less than all." That's not true on the LSAT. "Most" means "more than half," and on the LSAT, *that can certainly include "all."* So on the LSAT, a statement like "Most American Presidents have been men" is perfectly reasonable.

independently in more than one society. What's missing from the premises is that money was invented "independently in more than one society." In an assumption question, I always look for something in the conclusion but not the premises. If it's in the conclusion, and it didn't come from a premise, it came from an assumption.

> (A) Correct. This is an easy answer choice to almost skip past, but wait a second. If there is a society so isolated that it has no outside influences, and it uses money (which, remember, *was* invented)...then the conclusion makes sense; the invention must have been independent of any other society. And since other societies *also* use money, then money must have been invented in more than one society. Independently (no influence from the isolated country).
>
> (B) Incorrect. Irrelevant. Language is used as a basis for comparing and contrasting to money, but the conclusion is about money, not language. Money and language may have similarities, but that doesn't mean that information about how language came into being is enough to prove how money came into being. The passage itself tells us that money and language have their differences as well as their similarities.
>
> (C) Incorrect. Very similar to (B). This answer choice does nothing to substantiate the conclusion that money must have been developed independently in more than one society. The passage's conclusion is concerned with *money*, not those universal features of society that are *not* inventions (such as language).
>
> (D) Incorrect. Yet again...completely irrelevant. There reference in the passage to money's being "useful" is only in that opening sentence that serves to introduce the topic. "Usefulness" does not appear in the conclusion or any important part of the argument, which only concerns how money came to be invented. This is a common type of wrong answer choice on the LSAT. When you have a conclusion that is attempting to show whether or not something happened, information about "why" it happened (because it's so useful) isn't going to do the trick.
>
> (E) Incorrect. As we go down the answer choices here, they get less and less relevant – if you keep a firm eye on the conclusion, at least. Again, what is the conclusion about? How money came to be invented. What societies have chosen to do *since* it was invented has nothing to do with how it was invented.

Afterthoughts: Keep that conclusion in mind. The argument is based on the premise that money was invented, and the conclusion is that it was invented in more than one society independently. The obvious potential alternative is that it was invented in one place, and the idea spread from society to society. The correct answer will be the one that explains why the conclusion is better than the alternative. Answers that do not make that distinction – invented independently in more than one place vs. invented just once and spread – are pretty much guaranteed to be irrelevant.

There's a strong tendency to avoid answer choices that go "beyond the scope" of the passage, and with good reason – they're usually wrong. But in this question type, remember there's a missing assumption. We're *told* that something has been left out of the passage. So in this case, it is not a problem to choose an answer that refers to countries that are "geographically isolated" even though there's no reference to geographic isolation in the passage. It's not in the passage, because it was *assumed*. As long as it justifies the conclusion, it's ok. The only possibilities are that it was invented in one place and spread everywhere, or that it was invented in more than one place. The passage's conclusion is that it was invented in more than one place. (A) is correct because it eliminates the "spread everywhere" possibilities – as long as there are societies that don't get outside influence, then it couldn't have "spread" to those societies.

23. Forethoughts: The initial statement is simply a definition, used to introduce the topic. The "reasoning" is the leap between the premise (the last sentence, starting with the first "For") and the conclusion (the middle sentence, starting with "Ironicially"). Before I look at any answer choices, I'm going to ponder how the writer goes from "No one will say anything bad about public figures" to "No one in the public eye will have a *good* reputation." That seems to be a contradiction. If you think about it, though, it's not. Do you have one of those friends or relatives who has something good to say about everyone? The problem is, when someone never says anything *bad*, you can't believe any of the *good* things he or she says. So, my predicted answer will be something like: There's no "good" reputation except in comparison to "bad" reputations.

- (A) Incorrect. This is the converse of the conclusion. The conclusion is that if there ARE strong laws, then *nobody* can have a good reputation. That does not follow from (or imply) the statement that if there are NOT strong laws, then *everyone* can have a good reputation. Moreover, it doesn't provide a basis for believing why there should be *any* connection between libel laws and someone's reputation. Restating the conclusion another way, even if the restatement were valid (and the converse is *not* a valid deduction anyway), will not "justify the reasoning." We need a connection between the *premises* and the conclusion.

- (B) Incorrect. This principle seems to undermine the argument, if anything, by calling into question the premise that nobody would say anything bad about public figures. The bigger problem with this choice, though, is that the conclusion states that nobody would have a good reputation. To say that "some" (at least one) would have bad reputations does not justify that "none" of them would have a good reputation. Maybe some would have bad reputations and other would have good reputations.

(C) Incorrect. This choice does nothing to justify the leap from strong libel laws to nobody having a good reputation. This is the moral answer again. Watch the answer choices that are about what "should" happen when the passage is describing what "will" happen. Remember, as a general rule, "should" has nothing to do with it, unless somehow specifically justified by the premises.

(D) Incorrect. This answer choice really does nothing to connect libel laws to people's reputations. In fact, it doesn't reference good or bad reputations at all, so it's really hard to imagine how it can justify the conclusion that it's "impossible" to have a good reputation in a country with strong libel laws. If anything, it seems like it would be easier to get a good reputation in a country like this, because not many bad things are being said, for the reason given.

(E) Correct. Just when I was about to give up on my predicted answer, it shows up. If it's true that nobody can have a *good* reputation unless some people have *bad* reputations, and it's also true that in a country with strong libel laws nobody says anything bad about public figures, then in those countries, not only will nobody get a bad reputation, but nobody will have a good reputation, either (as the conclusion states). Essentially, everyone will have a "neutral" reputation. This is our link between the premise (nobody will say anything bad) and the conclusion (nobody will have a good reputation).

Afterthoughts: Think of the "reasoning" as the jump between the premise(s) and the conclusion. Questions that ask you to "justify" or "explain" the reasoning are asking you to account for that leap that always occurs between premise(s) and conclusion. How did the speaker get from A to B? Answer choices that may be true statements, or consistent with what the speaker might say, aren't going to be good enough if they don't provide the basis for that jump.

24. Forethoughts: This question type is asking for a conclusion, but it doesn't have to be a main conclusion that the passage could supply; a well-supported intermediate conclusion will do. Reading through the passage, it has a lot of premises and connections. There's just no efficient way to map through it all and predict an answer with any confidence. Instead, I'm going to be guided by the answer choices and see which of them is "strongly supported."

(A) Incorrect. Too strong. The passage says that mammals cannot "digest" cellulose, but for all I know, digestion isn't required to "obtain beneficial health effects." Additionally, this feels like a bad answer choice, because it really doesn't involve any inference or connecting of the premises. If this were correct answer would essentially be an interpretation of the first sentence; everything else in the passage about tumors, immune cells, beta-glucans, etc. would all be pointless. That seems unlikely.

(B) Incorrect. This is an invalid deduction. The passage tells us that if extracts from a mushroom can use cellulose to make beta-glucans, then it will slow/reverse/prevent cancer growth in mammals, but that does not mean if it slows/reverses/prevents cancer growth, then it must be using cellulose to create beta glucans. Uses Beta-Glucans → Stop Cancer; does not imply: Stop Cancer → Uses Beta-Glucans. Maybe using cellulose to create beta-glucans is simply one of several ways that mushrooms can help fight cancer (and the only way the passage teaches us about). Then if the mushroom fights cancer, it may be the beta-glucans, or it may be something else. We can't be sure.

(C) Correct. The phrase "degree of branching" leads me to the relevant portion of the passage. The antitumor activity increasing "as the degree of branching increases" means pretty much exactly what choice (C) states – more branching, more anti-tumor activity, and from the last sentence, we know that the "antitumor activity" is, specifically, increasing immune cell activity.

(D) Incorrect. We don't know what effects immune-cell activity *causes*. We're only told about immune-cell activity as an effect. 1) Extracts increase immune-cell activity. 2) Extracts do not kill cancer cells directly. That's it. The word "directly" is a word to pay special attention to. Always watch out of adverbs on the LSAT Logical Reasoning sections. (D) is incorrect because the passage doesn't tell us that *immune cell activity* doesn't kill cancer cells; it tells us that the *extracts* don't kill them (directly). Maybe the extracts kill cancer cells *indirectly* by getting the immune cells to do their dirty work. From the passage, it sounds like that's what's going on.

(E) Incorrect. Hopefully, "Any organism" caught your attention as being too strong. We're not told about "any organism." In fact, the *only* organism that we're told can obtain glucose from wood is mushrooms. So we know something about what mushrooms can do with it, but that's it. Maybe turnips can obtain glucose from wood, and wood has a different effect on them than it does on mushrooms. For any "non-mushroom," we'd be guessing. The passage doesn't tell us.

Afterthoughts: While predicting an answer is a very useful technique on the LSAT, it's not particularly helpful for some question types. In particular, the questions that ask you do draw inferences ("Which of the following is most strongly supported" "Which of the following must be true," etc.) are not good candidates for the prediction technique.

Forethoughts: The comparison is between manners and laws; unfortunately, as I scan the answer choices, I see that they all get that far. The question is going to be in what respect that comparison is being made. The comparison is that obeying the law, like exhibiting good manners, is done out of a sense of <u>custom</u>. It's not done for other reasons (specifically, not because of the <u>consequences</u> attached to not doing so). Seems straightforward enough: "to act otherwise would be uncustomary."

- (A) Incorrect. Not only is this choice not the main point of the argument, it is apparently being made up out of thin air. There's nothing at all in the passage about laws or manners varying from society to society. The question asks for something "*utilized by the argument*;" this is definitely *not* the time to go beyond the scope of the passage. It may be TRUE, but it's not coming from the passage.

- (B) Incorrect. Unlike (A), this answer choice actually uses the key terms and may trap an unsuspecting reader. The key to eliminating this answer choice is the word "adopting." There is nothing in the passage about why laws are *adopted*. The passage is concerned only with why laws are *obeyed*.

- (C) Correct. As long as you recognize that "compliance" is a synonym for obedience, this choice should be easy to spot. It is the one that addresses why the laws are followed, which is the point of the passage.

- (D) Incorrect. The reference to being "ethically required" is a bit of a trap, as the phrase does appear in the passage. However, the passage only considers being "ethically required" as a (discarded) possibility for why laws are followed; there's no parallel reference considering ethical requirements with respect to manners. Moreover, there's nothing in the passage that tells us what "most" laws do.

- (E) Incorrect. The passage does not say anything about whether the penalties involved are "strict," and you might have inferred that they're not, because the passage tells us that penalties aren't the reason people follow laws. But that's reading into the passage. Just because "fear of penalty" isn't the reason people follow laws, that doesn't mean the penalties aren't strict; it might just be that violating social custom is a more powerful motivator.

Afterthoughts: Not much on the way of takeaway points here; this is a pretty straightforward question if you read the passage carefully.

Section 2 (Logic Games[16])

GAME 1

This game is essentially a sequencing game, as things are happening in order (Monday morning comes before Monday afternoon, which comes before Tuesday morning, etc.), but it's really a hybrid, because we also have the grouping elements, dealing with the pairs of activities that take on each of the days. It seems like it will make the most sense to use a two-dimensional diagram (which I wouldn't do in a pure sequencing game) to acknowledge that grouping element. Off to the side, I make a "checklist" of all the information that is known, but that I can't place in the diagram with 100% certainty. Before I look at problem 1, my setup looks like this:

	Wed.	Thurs.	Fri.
Morn.			
Aft.			

J	or	J
K		Q

N	or	S
R		R

Q=earlier DAY than K and N

---

[16] Technically, the "Analytical Reasoning" section, but known by almost everyone as Logic Games

I emphasize "day" in the last rule to remind me that Q isn't just "earlier" than K and N; for instance, Q can't be in the morning and K in the afternoon on the same day, but if I just wrote "earlier", I might miss that.

1. Forethoughts: This is a typical "first question" in that it doesn't add any additional information; it simply asks about possible layouts based on the information we already have. The best way to do these questions is to just start with (A), and go systematically down the checklist. Don't skip around; take one answer choice at a time, checking each rule once. Here's how it shakes out:

- (A) Incorrect. Violates the rule that Quilting must be an earlier day than Kite-making.

- (B) **Correct.**

- (C) Incorrect. Violates the rule that Quilting must be an earlier *day* than Needlepoint.

- (D) Incorrect. Violates the rule that Rug-making must be in the afternoon.

- (E) Incorrect. Violates the rule that Jewelry must be in the morning.

Afterthoughts: In real life, under timed conditions, I wouldn't have analyzed (C), (D), or (E). I only have three rules to check; (B) satisfies those three rules, so after I look at (B), I'm done. It's a "Could Be True" question, so I'm going to trust the examiners and myself – if (B) could be true, then (C), (D), and (E) can't. If I save 10 seconds per answer choice by not looking at them, I've already got 30 "extra" seconds that will come in handy when I get to the third or fourth game.

2. Forethoughts: This is a "Must Be False" (MBF) question; in a "Must Be" question, sometimes you may be able to see the big picture – i.e., you know which one must be false (or true, if it's an "MBT" question). If not, though, don't panic; just work through the answer choices. The thing about a "Must Be" question, though, is that you want to test the *opposite* of what it's telling you. For instance, since this is an MBF question, I'm going to see if each answer choice, in turn, could be TRUE. The one that can't be true is the one that must be false.

- (A) So, in (A) for instance, I'm going to assume that Jewelry CAN be given on Thursday morning. If so, it's a wrong answer (If it *can be true*[17], it's not the one that MBF). Here's my diagram starting point, assuming that the statement in (A) is *true*:

---

[17] Ok, in case it's not obvious, from here on out: "Could Be True" = CBT. "Must Be True" = MBT. "Could Be False" = CBF. "Must Be False" = MBF.

	Wed.	Thurs.	Fri.
A.M.		J	
P.M.			

Since the question gives me information about Jewelry (J), I go to my rule about J, and I see that I have to make K or Q the Thursday afternoon choice. I'll try Q. This is arbitrary on my part; I'm trying to create *any* single layout that doesn't violate any rules (one valid layout is enough to show that Jewelry *could* be given on Thursday morning). Since I'm making an assumption about Q, I look for a Q rule; Q has to be on an earlier day than both K and N, so that puts K and N on Friday, which leaves R and S for Wednesday. R and S on Wednesday doesn't violate a rule, as long as S is in the morning. So, it's:

	Wed.	Thurs.	Fri.
A.M.	S	J	K
P.M.	R	Q	N

So answer choice (A) is <u>incorrect</u>. It *doesn't* have to be false that J is Thursday morning.

(B) I always look for chances to "cheat" and save time. Time saved now is points earned later. How does that help me here? Remember, the answer to question 1 was (B); that gave me a complete layout with K being given on Thursday morning. So, for question 2, I'm not going to do any new analysis for answer choice (B); I've already approved a layout showing that K could be Thursday morning, so (B) is <u>incorrect</u> – it CBT, so it doesn't have to be false. When you see what question 2 asks, you should immediately look to question 1 and see if you can eliminate an answer choice. If you didn't notice that question 1 elminated (B), the way you'd attack it is exactly the same way as (A), except instead of starting with J in the Thursday morning slot, you'd start with K there, instead. Then you work from that assumption; for instance, J has to be on an earlier day than K, so you'd put J on Wednesday. And so on, until you get to a valid layout that might just look a lot like (B) in question 1.

(C) If I look at the pairings that "worked" in (A), I can see if there's any way to rearrange them. The only sequential rule is that Q has to come before K and N. Since I have to put N on Thursday anyway, what if I move S/R to the end and shift everyone else forward one spot? I'd have to move N to the morning, but I don't have a rule that says I can't, so...

	Wed.	Thurs.	Fri.
A.M.	J	N	S
P.M.	Q	K	R

I go down my checklist to verify this possible layout, and I confirm that it doesn't violate any rules, so (C) is <u>incorrect</u>, and I eliminate it.

(D) The first step of creating a potential layout with Q on Thursday morning is easy – from my "Q rule," K and N have to be on Friday (Q must be on an earlier day than both). So my starting point is:

	Wed.	Thurs.	Fri.
A.M.		Q	K
P.M.			N

Since I just reached a conclusion about K and N, the next thing I do is look at rules about K or N, and I see that R has to be with N or S. But R can't be with N; K is with N. So R is with S.

	Wed.	Thurs.	Fri.
A.M.	S	Q	K
P.M.	R		N

That can only happen on Wednesday, which leaves Thursday afternoon as the only possible slot for J. But J has to be in the morning, so none of this can work. I've hit a contradiction by trying to put Q on Thursday morning and drawing the necessary inferences, so this is the one that CANNOT happen. **(D) is correct.**

(E) <u>Incorrect</u>. Again, under timed conditions, I wouldn't analyze (E). I know (D) is correct (since the layout is impossible), so I'd be on to question 3. Having said that, this might have been the first answer choice, in which case I'd have looked at it first, so it's good to know that I could have eliminated it. Using the same logic as in (C), as long as Q comes first and I keep the same pairings, I'm fine, so why not just switch Thursday and Friday? That gives me:

	Wed.	Thurs.	Fri.
A.M.	J	S	K
P.M.	Q	R	N

I run down the rules and see that no rule is violated by this layout, so S *can* be Thursday morning, and (as expected) (E) is incorrect.

3. Forethoughts: Same question type (MBF), so I'm going to work by process of elimination, getting rid of the ones that CBT, by simply plugging each answer choice in and seeing what happens.

- (A) Starting with J and K on Wednesday, I immediately look for my rules about J and K. The first rule is that J is in the morning, on the same day as K or Q. That rule is satisfied. I have another rule about K, though – Q has to be given on an earlier day than K. Clearly, that's impossible if K is on Wednesday, so the layout offered by answer choice A is impossible, which means that **(A) is correct.** J and K CANNOT be the ones given on Wednesday. Again, on the actual LSAT or during timed practice, this question is *over*. I'm on to #4 without looking at choices B, C, D, or E. If you don't like running out of time on question 18, look for opportunities to save time on question 3. This is a beautiful question, because it takes about 10-15 seconds, and you can be 100% certain that it's correct, as long as you have a good checklist. Clearly, there's no way that Quilting can be on an earlier day than Kite-making if Kite-making is on Wednesday. If I'd had to, here's how I could have eliminated the other options:

- (B) Time to cheat again! From the analysis of (E) on question 2, I already know that J/Q can be the Wednesday layout (also, question 1 answer choice (B)). Since J/Q is possible for Wednesday, (B) is incorrect. If you missed that, you'd just plug in J/Q for Wednesday (MBF question, so see if it CBT), and continue filling in the grid; here, there are a couple of possible layouts (including the one presented as answer choice (B) in question 1) – any one of them eliminates (B).

- (C) Starting with Q/S on Wednesday, I can see that my only sequential rule will automatically be satisfied (both K and N will have to come on a later day than Q). Next, J has to be with K or Q; in this case, that has to be K (Q is already spoken for). That leaves R and N, and the second rule tells me that they can go together. So one possible layout that disproves choice (C) is:

	Wed.	Thurs.	Fri.
A.M.	Q	J	N
P.M.	S	K	R

- (D) Starting with S/Q, again, the sequential rule will be satisfied. J has to be with K or Q; here, that will mean J with K. That leaves N and R, and just like in the previous answer choice, I know that works. This is just (C) with the Wednesday workshops flipped around:

	Wed.	Thurs.	Fri.
A.M.	S	J	N
P.M.	Q	K	R

(E) Starting with S/R, the diagram I created to evaluate 2.(A) shows that this is a possible layout, which eliminates (E) here, with no extra work. If I'd erased that diagram, or had to create it again, here's how I'd do it: I know that Q has to come before K and N. That puts both K and N on Friday, and leaves J/Q for Thursday:

	Wed.	Thurs.	Fri.
A.M.	S	J	K
P.M.	R	Q	N

So (E), too, is eliminated.

4. Here's a "CBT" question, which means I'll again test the answer choices the same way, but this time, as soon as I find one that works, I'm done (In a MBF question, when you find an answer choice that "works" (that is, one that could be true), you've eliminated it). All analysis starts with K in the "Friday Morning" position, plus whatever other piece of information I'm given in the answer choice. For instance:

(A) I start here:

	Wed.	Thurs.	Fri.
A.M.		J	K
P.M.			

I'm placing K from the question itself, and J by assumption, since I'm looking at answer choice (A). This time, I can cheat with no qualms whatsoever: See the diagram for 3E, immediately above – This is the last thing I did! I've just shown that Thursday and Friday morning can be J and K, respectively. If that diagram were erased, this would be easy to quickly create from the J/K shell – J has to be with K or Q. Can't be K, so I have to put Q on Thursday afternoon. Q has to come before K and N, which means that N has to be Friday afternoon. That leaves S/R for Wednesday, and voila – the 3E diagram is re-created. **(A) is correct**, and I'm on to question 5. Seriously. I'm not wasting *any* time looking at (B) through (E). But let's eliminate the others, for practice...

(B) Starting with K on Friday morning and N on Thursday afternoon. Q has to come on an earlier *day* than those two, which means Q is on Wednesday. So:

	Wed.	Thurs.	Fri.
A.M.	Q?		K
P.M.	Q?	N	

R has to be with N or S. None of the days has room for R *and* S, so R must be with N. But that won't work, either, because both R and N have to be in the afternoon. So I've hit a contradiction, and choice B must be wrong; this layout is impossible.

(C) Q on Wednesday morning, and K on Friday morning. J has to be in the morning, too, so that leaves only Thursday. But J has to be with K or Q, which is impossible if they're all on different days, so this answer choice won't work. Just to clarify, when I'm working this problem, I'm not just *thinking* about it – I'm writing out a little grid with Q and K in place, then writing down the J (from the first rule on the checklist), then looking at the second half of that rule, and seeing from my diagram that it's impossible.

(D) K on Friday morning, R on Friday afternoon. Since the answer choice gives me information about R, I look to my checklist for a rule about R. Found one! R has to be on the same day as N or S. So R can't be with K, and this answer choice is wrong.

(E) K on Friday morning, and S on Wednesday afternoon. S is tied to my rule about R, so I'll start there – R has to be in the afternoon with N or S. But I've put S in the afternoon, so R can't be with S. R must be with N, and the only day that has room for R and N is Thursday. Now I'm up to:

	Wed.	Thurs.	Fri.
A.M.		N	K
P.M.	S	R	

Q has to come before N and K, so that puts Q on Wednesday morning, which leaves only Friday afternoon for J. But J has to be in the morning. So I've hit a contradiction that can't be resolved, and (E) is wrong, also.

Afterthoughts: A great way to avoid that deer-in-headlights thing and to always know where you're going next is to be guided by the questions themselves and the answer choices. It's a real time-saver. If the question gives you information about a variable, you should immediately look for rules that involve that variable. If not, or after you've done that, then when you're testing answer choices, look for rules that involve the answer choice you're looking at. (D) could have been eliminated in 5 seconds, if need be, by just starting out by looking for a rule about R. But if you take an unsystematic approach, and just try to fill out the rest of the diagram, you could end up messing around with (D) for much longer than you should.

5. Forethoughts: As it turns out, this one provides enough information (mostly because it's about Q, a highly-restricted variable) to work out the entire layout without hammering on the individual answer choices. The question gives more information about Q, so I immediately check my Q rules. I see that J has to be in the morning, either with K or Q. But since Q has to be in the morning for this question, that means it's going to be J/K. That leaves N, Q, R, and S. Who can Q be paired with? Well, R has to be with N or S, so Q can't be with R. Q also can't be with N, because Q has to come on an earlier day than N. So Q is with S, and N is with R. So the pairs are: J/K, Q/S (either order order), and N/R. Because Q has to come on an earlier day than both K *and* N (which are on different days), Q/S has to be on Wednesday. So **Answer Choice E is correct** – Scrapbooking cannot be on Thursday. Here are the layouts that show that the other answer choices are wrong, because the answer choices they relate to CAN take place on Thursday:

	Wed.	Thurs.	Fri.
A.M.	Q	J	N
P.M.	S	K	R

This shows that answer choices (A) and (B) are wrong, because either Jewelry or Kite-making could be on Thursday.

	Wed.	Thurs.	Fri.
A.M.	Q	N	J
P.M.	S	R	K

Similarly, this layout eliminates answer choices (C) and (D), because either Needlepoint or Rug-making could be on Thursday.

6. The simplest way to do one of these types of questions is to just try each variable in turn. As soon as you get one possible layout that works for a variable, you can move on to the next one. Of course, you want to check the diagrams you've already created, to save time. For instance, the last diagram in question 5, above, shows that Q can be Wednesday morning. Because R has to be on an afternoon, I know that R is out. That leaves J, K, N, and S. Let's see which, if any, could be on Wednesday morning.

Not K or N; they each have to come on a later day than Q, so they can't be on Wednesday. So the only ones I have to test are J and S. Let's start with J. J has to be on the same day as K or Q. I'm trying to create any layout that works. Does it matter whether I try to put K or Q in the Wednesday afternoon slot? Well, yeah...K can't come before Q. So if it's at all possible to put J on Wednesday morning, it will have to be with Q on Wednesday afternoon:

	Wed.	Thurs.	Fri.
A.M.	J		
P.M.	Q		

Next step: R has to be in the afternoon with N or S. ok, how about N on Thursday? Seems to work fine:

	Wed.	Thurs.	Fri.
A.M.	J	N	K
P.M.	Q	R	S

So J and Q can be on Wednesday morning, and R, K, and N can't. The last one to try is S. Since I'm trying S, I'm immediately looking for a rule that pertains to S. Either S or N has to be in the morning with R. Well, I was going to put S in the morning anyway, so I'll plug it in with R and see if it works:

	Wed.	Thurs.	Fri.
A.M.	S		
P.M.	R		

Q has to come before K and N, so that pretty much puts Q and J on Thursday, and K and N on Friday:

	Wed.	Thurs.	Fri.
A.M.	S	J	K
P.M.	R	Q	N

A quick check shows that this layout doesn't violate any rules, so **(C) is correct** – 3 of them can be on Wednesday morning: Q, S, and J. The other three can't – R, because it has to be on an afternoon, and K & N, because they have to come after Q.

GAME 2

Every LSAT-taker's best friend – the pure sequencing game. The "diagram" couldn't be simpler: 1   2   3   4   5   6

Additionally, here's my checklist, for the information that's not 100% (e.g. something like "Bob appears 4th" would go right into the diagram, with a "B" under the "4." Other information makes a checklist that I can just run down to confirm or eliminate answer choices). Here's what it looks like:

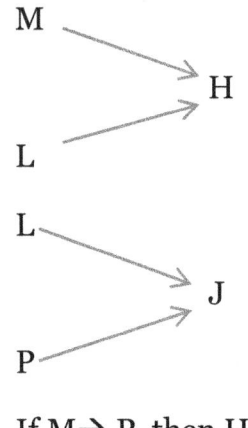

If M → P, then H → G

If G → H, then P → M

G ≠ 6

Each of these bits should be easy to correlate to the clues, except for: "If G → H, then P → M." This is the contrapositive of the rule immediately before it. WHENEVER you have a conditional rule in a logic game, record the contrapositive as soon as you get the rule down. Although the contrapositive is usually phrased in the negative, because of the content of this came, the contrapositive can be written affirmatively. The "pure" contrapositive would be "If H DOES NOT appear earlier than G, then M DOES NOT appear earlier than P. But here, everyone is in a line, one after the other. So "H does not appear earlier than G" means that G appears earlier than H. Similarly, "M does not appear earlier than P" means that P appears earlier than M. Here, there are only two possibilities – G is before H or H is before G. Similarly with P and M.

Also, notice, I don't bother writing "Not G" under the 6 in my main diagram. I don't like to clutter the diagram with information that's not 100%. That's what the checklist is for. I get the basic information down in the diagram or the checklist, then I move onto the questions and the answer choices. For an excellent look at a different approach – doing a comprehensive job of analyzing the game at the outset – see <u>LSAT Logic Games</u>

Solution Manual, by Morley Tatro, available through www.cambridgelsat.com or www.amazon.com.

7. Again, the typical first question that adds no information. The best approach is to start with (A), and run it by your checklist, then (B), (C), etc. until you find the one that doesn't violate any rules. Systematic. If you've accurately translated the rules to your checklist, these questions are free points and added time on the clock.

    (A) Violates the rule that Paredes (P, and so on with the others) appears before J.

    (B) Violates the rule that if M appears before P, then H appears before G.

    (C) Violates the rule that L (and M, for that matter) must appear before H.

    (D) Violates the rule that G does not appear last.

    (E) **Correct.**

After eliminating (A) through (D), circle (E) without spending a moment evaluating it. There's only one right answer; if you've found the 4 wrong ones, you're done.

8. This is a "MBF" question, so I'm going to test the answer choices by seeing if they CBT. The 4 that can are eliminated. For each answer choice, I'm just trying to create one single layout that doesn't violate any of the rules.

    (A) H is before (→) G. I'm just trying to create any layout at all where this can be true. I notice that a couple of actors have to come before H, so I'd better get them in first. Here's my initial try:

1	2	3	4	5	6
L	M	H			

I'm just taking care of that first rule, and also making sure I get H down in such a way that I know he'll come before G. Next, I see that P has to come before J, and G can't be last. So the last 3 could be P-G-J. That should work.

1	2	3	4	5	6
L	M	H	P	G	J

No rules are violated by this layout, so H *can* come before G. (A) is incorrect.

    (B) The starting point is easy; H is 6. Looking at my rules about H, the first rule will be satisfied automatically. I have another rule about H: If G is before H (and he will be), then P is before M. Another rule I have to take care of is L and P have to be before J. I want P to be early anyway (to get in there before M). So if I drop a few in, I might get:

1	2	3	4	5	6
L	P				H

That's going to take care of a lot. L and P are already before J, and L and M are already before H. G is not last, and P will be before M. It looks like I can do whatever I want with the others. For instance:

1	2	3	4	5	6
L	P	M	G	J	H

This doesn't violate any rules, so H *can* be 6th, and (B) is wrong.

(C) Starting point: L is 5. Looking at the first rule about L, I see that L has to come before H, so H must be 6. But the next rule says that L has to come before J, also, and there's no more room to put J after L. L can't be 5 and have both H *and* J after him. That's the one that CANNOT be true, so **(C) is correct**. On the actual LSAT, or during timed practice, there's absolutely no reason to look at (D) or (E). But since we're here...

(D) Looking at the diagram I've created for (B), above, I see that it demonstrates that P can come before M, so (D) is wrong. If I had to start from scratch, I'd put L and P early. I'd also put M early, since he has to come before J; I just wouldn't put him before P. So, "L-P-M" (or P-L-M, just as easily) at 1-2-3 would be a good start, and I'd be well on my way to making a diagram like: L-P-M-G-J-H, which shows that P *can* appear before M, and therefore (D) is incorrect.

(E) Also looking at the same diagram, I see that P can be second, so (E) is wrong. I swear, I didn't do that on purpose. Sometimes you get lucky, and one layout knocks out 3 (or 4) wrong answer choices. If you had to attack this one from scratch, your starting point would be to place P in the 2-slot, and go from there.

Afterthoughts: When you're creating layouts to prove (or disprove) answer choices, you're just trying to find one that works, so don't agonize too much about who has to be where. For instance, in evaluating (E), above, the only thing you *know* you have to do is put P second. How do you go from there, efficiently? Let the rules guide you. Both H and J need a couple of specific guys in front of them, so make it easy on yourself: Put them at 5 and 6, and those first two rules will automatically be satisfied – you won't have to worry about it again. Plus, the rule that G can't be 6 will be satisfied, too. Now you're certainly well on your way. You also have a rule that imposes consequences if M is before P. Don't let that rule slow you down at all – just put P before M, instead. Now that rule doesn't apply. And so on. The layouts you construct are up to you, but do it in such a way that you're not fighting the rules; that's how you eliminate 'false starts' (when you get to a point where the diagram you're working on won't work, but you're not sure if maybe another one will).

9. Forethoughts: Again (see Question 6 from game 1), the key to these "How many?" questions is just to check each variable, systematically. That's best for both speed *and* accuracy, and really, how else would you do it? The thing to avoid is a haphazard, generalized jumping around. Let's take the easy ones first. G can't be 6; we have a rule that prohibits it directly. L and M can't be 6; they have to come earlier than H, and you can't be earlier than anyone if you're #6. P can't be 6; he has to be before J. So right off the bat, the only possibilities are H and J. Looking at a couple of the diagrams that were created for 8), above, I notice that I've already shown that both H and J can, in fact, be #6, so **(D) is correct**: Two of them can be #6 – H and J.

But let's say I'd erased the diagram where J was 6. How would I come to the right answer? I'd test it by putting J in the 6-slot. This satisfies a couple of rules right away – G is not last, and both L and P will have to be before J. The next rule I'd look at is the first – L and M have to come before H, so why not put them 1 and 2? Now I'm up to:

	1	2	3	4	5	6
	L	M				J

The only rule I haven't covered is the conditional. M is going to come before P, so I have to put H before G. Easy enough. How about:

	1	2	3	4	5	6
	L	M	H	G	P	J

So J can be 6. Even if I'd erased the diagram where H was 6, I may notice that by eliminating (B) on question 8, I've already concluded that H can be 6. A number of layouts prove this, for instance answer choice (E) to question 7: P-M-L-J-G-H.

10. Odd question…we know that J has to be before M, but we don't know where, and the answer choices give us the other 4, but we don't know where (and they don't have to be consecutive; they just have to be in the given relative order). I'm just going to lay out the chain in each answer choice, without worrying about the numbers, and see if I can drop in J and M in such a way that it works. Remembering that for each possible layout, J must come before M.

(A) Start: G-L-P-H

From the beginning...M has to be before H, and P has to be before J. The only way to meet those two requirements is to drop JM in between the P and the H. That gives me:

1	2	3	4	5	6
G	L	P	J	M	H

Let's check the rules. I had the first two rules in mind when I tried this layout; they're ok. The conditional rule doesn't apply, because M is not before P (when you know a conditional rule doesn't apply, you don't have to check the contrapositive). Finally, G is not last. Sometimes you get lucky and **(A) is correct**. In real life, I wouldn't look at the other answer choices – since we're here, though...

(B) Start: G-P-H-L

The first rule is that L has to be before H, so this choice is incorrect.

(C) Start: L-H-G-P

Again, taking the rules in order, L and M have to be before H. L already is, so that part's easy. But now I also need M (and J, which comes before M) before H. But P has to come before J. So I have 3 rules that are in conflict here – if I put J after P (second rule) and M before H (first rule), then there's no way I can have J before M (condition of question #10). (C) is incorrect.

(D) Start: L-P-H-G

M has to come before H (rule 1) and P has to come before J (rule 2). That's only possible if the JM pair is placed in between P and H, so:

1	2	3	4	5	6
L	P	J	M	H	G

But that all puts G in the 6-slot, which violates the last rule, so (D) is incorrect.

(E) Start: P-L-H-G

M has to come before H, and P has to come before J (again, rules 1 and 2). Now, if I'm paying attention after the work on answer choice (D), I'll realize that means J and M have to be in between P and H (with L in there somewhere), and the details don't really matter anymore – after I put J and M before H, once again, G will be last, and that's not permitted. So answer choice (E) is incorrect, also.

11. Forethoughts: An "MBT" question. If the conditions of the question don't provide an "ah ha!" moment, I'll work through the answer choices, but this time, since it's a "Must Be" question, I'll have to see if they could be *false*. Remember, if you're testing answer choices on a "Must Be" questions, you always check the opposite. So far, we've seen "Must Be *False*" questions, so we've been testing to see whether the individual answer choices are *true*. Here, though, we have a "Must Be *True*" question, so we need to see whether each individual answer choice could be *false*. The one that can't be falsified is the right answer.

What I would do here is take a quick look at the variables affected by the conditions (L and G), and see if that might suggest a likely candidate to test first. That may save me some time instead going down the list from (A) to (E) in order. Here, for instance, the rules about L apply to L and someone else (M in the first rule, and P in the second rule) coming before both H and J. So if I also attach G to L, then H and J are coming even *later*. So my guess without doing any analysis would be that answer choice (B) is the most likely. I could be wrong, but I'm going to try them out of order. If (B) is wrong, I'll get to (A) later.

- (B) As I said in the intro, I'm going to test H *not* being last. (see if it could be *false* that H is last). If the question were which *could be true*, I would put H at 6 and see if I could create a layout that worked. That won't help here, because showing that H *could* be last wouldn't tell me that he *must* be last. But if I can put him anywhere else, then I'll have DISproved the answer choice. I know that H has to come pretty late (L, M, and now G have to come before H), so to show that he could be somewhere other than 6, I'm going to see if H can be 5. I know that L and G have to be together, in that order, and L also has to be ahead of J, so it seems like I should try to put L first. My starting point will be:

1	2	3	4	5	6
L	G			H	

From the conditional clue, P has to come before M, because G is coming before H. P also has to come before J. So it looks like P has to be 3. Contrary to my expectations, I think this layout is going to work:

1	2	3	4	5	6
L	G	P	M	H	J

Running down the checklist, I see that this layout *does* work, so answer choice (B) is eliminated. My hope was that putting H outside of the 6-slot would fail, which would mean that (B) is the right answer, but it didn't work out that way. Looking at the other answer choices, (C) actually looks obvious – I know that L has to come early. I'll analyze that one next.

(C) Again, I'm looking at trying to falsify the answer choices, which means the issue is whether L can come later than third (as opposed to the question, which says "*no* later")? Let's try 4th. That means only two of them could be after L (5 and 6). But H (rule 1), J (rule 2), and G (additional information from question 11) all have to come after L. So, indeed, it must be true that L appears no later than 3rd, and **(C) is correct**. At least I saved time by not looking at (A). The idea is this – I'm looking for something that "must be true," so I may as well start with answer choices that I know offer things that are most likely to be true. From the earlier problems and the rules, I know that H has to come pretty late (remember, only H or J can be 6 (question 9)). I also know that L has to come pretty early. So it makes sense to give (B) and (C) a try first. Let's look at how we could have eliminated the other wrong answers, if we had to (of course, in a timed test, I would not have looked at A, D, or E):

(A) Again, testing the opposite (since it's a "must be" question), I want to try to put G *later* than 3. He's going to have to come pretty early if he's glommed onto L, so I'll try him at 4. Starting with:

```
1    2    3    4    5    6

              L    G
```

L has to come before H and J, so they're going to occupy the last two spots, in either order. That puts M and P in the first two slots. Since G will be before H, I'll have to put P before M (conditional rule). That means:

```
1    2    3    4    5    6

P    M    L    G    H    J
```

No rules are violated, so (A) is incorrect: G *can* appear later than third.

(D) The starting point is to put G somewhere before M (to falsify (D)). I know that L always has to come early, and L and G are attached (from the question), so I'm going to start with:

```
1    2    3    4    5    6

L    G    M
```

Running down the checklist, I see that this start will automatically satisfy the first and last rules, but it messes me up on the conditional rule. If G is before H, then P has to be before M. So I have to get P up there in front of M. Next try:

1	2	3	4	5	6
L	G	P	M		

Now I've satisfied the first and last rules, and I don't have to worry about the conditional rule (since M isn't before P anymore). I've also satisfied the second rule, since whether J is 5 or 6, it will be after L and P. Filling in the blanks:

1	2	3	4	5	6
L	G	P	M	H	J

So M does not have to appear earlier than G, and (D) is incorrect.

(E) The diagram I just finished for (D) shows that (E) is incorrect, also – it need not be true that P appears first.

Afterthoughts: When you're creating these quick charts to verify or disprove answer choices, you're just looking for one that works. You have to make assumptions and see what might work. If you get to a spot where one doesn't work, you have to figure out whether it doesn't work because due to the rules it *can't* work, or whether it doesn't work because of one of the assumptions you made, in which case you have to modify your assumption and move on.

For instance, look at how I worked on (D) – I made an assumption that the starting point was LGM, and then I saw that I had violated the conditional rule. That didn't mean that (D) was correct, though; it meant that my initial assumption about starting with LGM wasn't going to work. So I had to tinker with it and sneak P up in front of M; that way, I no longer had to deal with the conditional rule. LGM wasn't set in stone; I just put them up there because I knew L and M had to come earlier than H (first rule). But they didn't *have* to come before P, so I was able to rework my initial assumption.

12. Forethoughts: Two ways to get to the right answer here – the "flash of inspiration" way, and the "grinding it out" way. You can actually help your chances of getting inspired – here's how to get this question right in 20 seconds or less: My starting point is M = 1. Since I'm given information about M, the first thing I do is look to my checklist for rules about M. M has to come before H; that's automatic if M = 1. There's also the conditional rule. If M is before P, (which will happen, since M = 1), then H is before G. So H has to be before G. But if I remember question 9, I know that only H and J can be last. *If H is going to be before G*, H can't be last...so J must be. That's answer choice (C), and it Must Be True, so **(C) is correct**..

If I don't catch that connection, though, no problem. It's a "MBT" question, so I'll work the answer choices and see if they could be false. The starting point is always M = 1.

(A) I'm going to assume that G is something *other than* 5. From the last rule, I know G can't be 6, and from the conditional rule, G has to come after H. I'm going to try to put G 4th. H has to come after both L and M, so in addition to M=1, I'll have to put L early, too. I'll try starting like this:

1	2	3	4	5	6
M	L	H	G		

All of the rules other than the second one are already satisfied. For the second rule, all I need to do is put P before J, so:

1	2	3	4	5	6
M	L	H	G	P	J

Since G *doesn't* have to be 5th (G can be 4th), (A) is incorrect.

(B) To analyze this choice, I need to move H off of the third position. I like M and L coming early, since they have to be ahead of H anyway, and I like J coming last. It looks like I can just bump H and G down one spot, and bring P up to 3:

1	2	3	4	5	6
M	L	P	H	G	J

All of the rules are satisfied, so H does not have to be third, and (B) is incorrect.

(C) Now I have to try to put J somewhere other than sixth. If I try to put J 5th, I start like this:

1	2	3	4	5	6
M				J	

The answer choice gave me information about J, so I go to my checklist for rules about J, and I see that L and P have to come before J. L also has to come before H, so I may as well put L at #2:

1	2	3	4	5	6
M	L			J	

The conditional clue tells me that H has to come before G, and G can't be last. So H and G would have to be 3 and 4, but I still have to put P before J, also. That's not going to work. In trying this layout, I've made some assumptions; is there anything I can change to make it work? Well, the problem I ran into was trying to fill up that 6-spot. M and L can't be 6; they have to come before H. P can't be 6; P has to come before J. That leaves H, G, and J. G can't be 6, from the last rule, and H can't be 6 – from the conditional rule, H has to come before G. So only J can be 6, and **(C) is correct**.

(D) L has to come early. He can't be #1, from the question's condition (M is 1), and I'm testing to see if it can be something other than #2, so I'll try it at #3. Starting point:

1	2	3	4	5	6
M		L			

Someone else who has to appear early is P (has to get in there before J, anyway). No reason not to see if P can be #2. Then 4 & 5 would have to be H and G, since H has to come before G (conditional clue), and G can't be last. That would give me:

1	2	3	4	5	6
M	P	L	H	G	J

This layout works, so (D) is wrong – L does not have to be second; L can be third.

(E) The diagram I just did for (D) also proves that (E) is incorrect – P does not have to be fourth; P can be second (or third or fifth, from the layouts created to analyze answer choices (B) and (A), respectively).

GAME 3

There might be a tendency to make the setup harder than it is. This is a sequencing game, but instead of 7 different letters, I only need two (different ones): MMM and SSSS. Don't complicate it; the diagram start is just:

```
    1   2   3   4   5   6   7
                    (M)
```

I put the M in parenthesis to remind me that 5=M is a permanent fixture of this game. As you've seen from the earlier games, I tend to make and remake a lot of quick diagrams; for space constraints, sometimes they get erased. I want to remind myself that 5 is *always* M, so I'd better not erase it. It's not just a quick assumption that I'm making to test an answer choice. M goes straight into the diagram because the rule gives me 100% information about 5 being M. Contrast with Game 2, when I didn't have any 100% information placing a particular variable in a particular location; in that case, everything went into the checklist. Here, the checklist is:

*3M and 4S

*Clean Between *different* loads

*Clean 1-3 times

There's really no efficient way to symbolize a couple of those clues; sometimes, you just have to write out little sentences.

13. Forethoughts: It seems like the key to all of the problems in this game will the limitation on the number of cleanings. There just aren't any other restrictions. This is a Could Be True question, which is the easiest type to evaluate – plug in the information in the answer choices and look for the one that doesn't lead to a contradiction.

(A)

```
    1   2   3   4   5   6   7
    M   S   M   S   M   S   S
```

There are only three M loads. The game starts with one at 5, and this answer choice puts the others at 1 and 3, so this is the only possible layout for (A). Now I'm just counting cleanings, and there are five: Between 1 & 2, 2 & 3, 3 & 4, 4 & 5, and 5 & 6 (the "different" loads, where we switch from M to S or vice versa). So (A) is wrong. One thing I can tell from looking at (A) that will probably speed me up in later questions is that valid layouts will only be possible when M's or S's are grouped together; when they're separated like this, I need too many cleanings.

(B)

1	2	3	4	5	6	7
S	M	M	S	M	S	S

Only four cleanings this time (between 1 & 2, 3 & 4, 4 & 5, and 5 & 6), because a couple of the M's are together. That's still too many, though, so (B) is incorrect.

(C)

1	2	3	4	5	6	7
S	M	S	S	M	M	S

Again, four cleanings. (between 1 & 2, 2 & 3, 4 & 5, and 6 & 7). So (C) is incorrect.

(D)

1	2	3	4	5	6	7
S	S	M	S	M	M	S

And again, four: (between 2 & 3, 3 & 4, 4 & 5, 6 & 7). (D) is incorrect.

(E)

1	2	3	4	5	6	7
S	S	S	M	M	M	S

In real life, I wouldn't look at answer choice (E). I've eliminated the other four, so I'd circle (E) and move on to question 14. But this is what the layout for (E) looks like, and sure enough, there are only two cleanings (between 3 & 4, and 6 & 7). So **(E) is correct**.

Afterthoughts: One very useful skill in the Logic Games section is the ability to figure out early on how the game is likely to resolve, i.e. what "key rules" seem to dictate whether most of the answer choices are eliminated or verified, etc. Coming to an early realization such as here – the layouts are only going to work when the loads are clumped together (look at (E), with its two groupings of three identical loads) will save you time and headaches later. If possible, try to get a feel for how the game works; don't just bounce from question to question and have to figure it all out from scratch each time.

14. I don't like to spend too much time thinking about questions in a general sense; that's a good way to make no progress while the clock ticks. Sometimes, I may feel that I'm going to have a flash of inspiration, and in those cases, I may take up to about 15 seconds or so looking for a "big picture" moment, but for the most part, I'm just trying to rip through the answer choices in a very systematic fashion. Here, again, that's what I'd do, and since it's a "must be true" question, I'm going to assume that each is false, and work from there until I find the one that I can't disprove. If a particular answer choice suggests itself to me, though, I'm happy to tackle them out of order. Looking at the options here, I'm really inclined to think that (D) or (E) is correct. I know that the key to avoiding the cleanings is to have groups of the same material hauled consecutively. I think I'll just start with (E) and work backwards.

- (E) Again, I'm trying to disprove this answer choice by assuming it's false. If I assume that it's NOT the case that three loads of stone are hauled consecutively, the best chance I have of coming up with a layout that works would probably be to do two loads of stone together twice. Something like:

1	2	3	4	5	6	7
S	S	M	M	M	S	S

    That doesn't violate any rules. In fact, I only used two cleanings; I had one to spare. So, (E) is incorrect – I don't HAVE to have three loads of stone in a row. So much for trying the answer choices from back to front?

- (D) Testing to see if this is false means that not even two loads of mulch are hauled in a row – they're all separated by at least one load of stone. That seems like it couldn't possibly work. I guess the best way to try it would be to put a bunch of loads of stone in a row, like maybe 2-3-4. So that would mean:

1	2	3	4	5	6	7
M	S	S	S	M	S	M

    That's still one cleaning too many, and moving one of the M's off of the endpoints (1 and 7) is just going to make it worse (the one on 5 can't move, from the final initial rule). For instance, switch 1 and 2, above:

1	2	3	4	5	6	7
S	M	S	S	M	S	M

    That just made it worse. I've gone from 4 cleanings to 5. **Answer choice (D) is correct.** There's just no way to follow all the rules and separate all of the M's.

In this case, having a feel for the game (and the need to group the similar materials together) guided me toward the later answer choices, and saved me time analyzing the earlier ones. If I hadn't had that sort of inspiration, though, here's how I would have eliminated the other answer choices:

(A) This is an easy answer choice to work through. I'm assuming the opposite (i.e. that it's NOT true that the second load is stone), so my starting point is easy:

```
   1    2    3    4    5    6    7
        M              M
```

(If the second load isn't stone, it's mulch). From here, the best way to make this layout work (I'm always trying to create possible layouts that work (i.e. don't violate any rules)) is to make #1 mulch, also – I've figured out that connecting the similar loads helps to ensure that I'm not violating the "three cleanings maximum" rule). So:

```
   1    2    3    4    5    6    7
   M    M    S    S    M    S    S
```

Sure enough, that holds the cleanings to exactly 3 (between 2 & 3, 4 & 5, and 5 & 6). So the second load *doesn't* need to be stone, and answer choice (A) is incorrect.

(B) This answer choice asks me if 1 and 2 have to be the same material, so instead I'm going to try to see if they could be different materials. What would be the best way to make that work? Well, I want as many in a row as possible, so if 1 and 2 have to be different, maybe I could make 2, 3, and 4 the same? That would have to be stone, since mulch is 5. So I'll start like:

```
   1    2    3    4    5    6    7
   M    S    S    S    M
```

Since I don't want to violate the three-cleanings rule, the second mulch should be #6 (next to the one at 5) and not #7. If I drop it there, I get:

```
   1    2    3    4    5    6    7
   M    S    S    S    M    M    S
```

Looks like 3 cleanings: Between 1 & 2, 4 & 5, and 6 & 7. So the first and second loads DON'T have to be the same material, and (B) is incorrect.

(C) This choice asks if the second and third loads have to be different. I just created a layout for (B) which shows that the second and third layouts can be the same. So (C) is incorrect, based on work I've just done.

15. For this question, in addition to the fifth load being mulch, the third load also has to be mulch. So my starting point is:

1	2	3	4	5	6	7
		M		M		

From here, since it's a "Must Be True" question, I'll be trying the *opposite* of whatever information I'm given for each answer choice, to see if each choice in turn "Could Be False" (thereby disproving it).

(A) The question asks if 6 & 7 have to be different. That means I'm going to see if they could be the same. If they're the same, they can't both be mulch; I only have one mulch load left, so if I'm to disprove this answer choice, it will be by creating a layout where both 6 and 7 are stone. So my starting point is:

1	2	3	4	5	6	7
		M		M	S	S

What's my best chance for making this layout work? Clearly by making the 4th load mulch, also. Keeping the similar loads together, as much as possible, is the way to avoid violating the three-cleanings rule. So:

1	2	3	4	5	6	7
S	S	M	M	M	S	S

This works easily – only needs two cleanings. So the 6th and 7th loads *don't* have to be different, and (A) is incorrect.

(B) The layout I just created for (A) disproves (B) as well – the first and second loads don't have to be different; here's one example showing that they could be the same. So (B) is incorrect, as well. When you create a layout that knocks out multiple answer choices, take advantage of it!

(C) (and (D), respectively). I hope you were paying attention – that first layout also disproves both (C) and (D) – loads 6 and 7 do not need to be mulch; they could both be stone. So (C) and (D) are wrong, and by process of elimination, **Answer**

Choice (E) is correct. I don't even need to analyze it, and I wouldn't waste the time to do so; the other possibilities have all been disproven. But if I looked at (E) first or something, here's how that analysis would go:

(E) This answer choice tests a specific layout – I know that 3 and 5 are M; the question is whether 1 could be M, also. If not, then it "must be true" that it's stone. So I lay out:

1	2	3	4	5	6	7
M	S	M	S	M	S	S

And I simply count the cleanings – five. That violates the three-cleanings-maximum rule, so I know that the first load cannot be mulch, which means it Must Be True that it's Stone, so (E) is correct.

16. Just when you thought it was tricky to have no more than three washings, now we're down to two. That means it's going to be even more important to group the similar loads together. No real trick to the question, though; again, it's a MBT, so plug in the opposite of each answer choice to see if it Could Be False. The one that can't be false is the right answer.

(A) Starting point:

1	2	3	4	5	6	7
	M			M		

From here, can I get to a layout that only has two cleanings? The only question is, where should I put the third M? The best try has to be in the 1-slot; that gets two M's in a row and means no cleaning until the 2/3 gap. However:

1	2	3	4	5	6	7
M	M	S	S	M	S	S

That puts two S's in a row twice, and two M's in a row once, and it still requires 3 cleanings (2-3, 4-5, and 5-6). It's impossible to get three M's OR S's in a row…I'm pretty comfortable saying it's not going to work with M in the 2-slot, which means it Must Be True that the second load is stone, and **Answer Choice (A) is correct**. If you have a good feel for a game, you don't necessarily have to try every single permutation (here, that would mean 5 possibilities – along with 2 and 5, the other M could be at 1, 3, 4, 6, or 7). But from the way the previous questions have panned out, and logically, understanding how the game works, I can tell that if it doesn't work with the third M at 1, it's just not going to work anywhere. For the belt and suspenders approach, I could tell myself it's probably (A), but I want to check (B) through (E) to make sure (though I think it's probably not worth the time investment).

(B) Starting point:

	1	2	3	4	5	6	7
			S		M		

What's the best way to make things work from here? Well, I could put a few S's in a row to start, then a few M's in a row after that:

	1	2	3	4	5	6	7
	S	S	S	M	M	M	S

Two cleanings, exactly (between 3-4 and 6-7). So the third load does NOT have to be mulch, and (B) is incorrect.

(C) Starting point:

	1	2	3	4	5	6	7
			M		M		

Having three M's in a row worked out pretty well for (B), so I'm just going to try (M) at 3, 4, and 5:

	1	2	3	4	5	6	7
	S	S	M	M	M	S	S

Again, two cleanings: between 2-3 and 5-6. So the third load doesn't have to be stone, either, and (C) is incorrect.

(D) The previous layout, which disproved (C), also disproves (D) – the sixth layout does not have to be mulch, so (D) is incorrect – no additional work required; just have to remember to look back. But <u>note</u> – I can't use the layouts I've done for previous questions, *unless they also satisfy the Question 16 requirement that there are exactly two cleanings.*

(E) The previous layout also shows me that (E) is incorrect – the seventh load does not have to be mulch, because I've created a layout that works where the seventh load is stone. So (E) is incorrect, also.

17. Last question...no 3 loads in a row. It's a Could Be True question, so it should be straightforward – assume each answer choice is true, then try to create a layout to prove it. Four will lead to contradictions; the one that doesn't is the right answer.

(A) Starting point:

	1	2	3	4	5	6	7
	S				M		

If I can't do three loads in a row, then I'll need to do as many two-in-a-rows as I can. The first 3 can't all be S...what if I make 2 and 3 both M?

	1	2	3	4	5	6	7
	S	M	M	S	M	S	S

Four cleanings...fail! What if just make #2 M?

	1	2	3	4	5	6	7
	S	M	S		M		

I'm up to two cleanings for sure already, and wherever I put the third M is going to create at least two more. This isn't working. What if just #3 is M?

	1	2	3	4	5	6	7
	S	S	M	S	M		

#4 can't be M, because I can't have 3 in a row, so I was able to fill that one in, too. But I'm up to three cleanings already, and as soon as I drop the last S in there, I'll have a fourth. (A) is incorrect; it can't be true that the first load is stone. That means I can add M=1 to my diagrams as I evaluate the other answer choices – if the first load can't be stone, it must be mulch.

(B) Starting point:

	1	2	3	4	5	6	7
	M			S	M		

Can this be true? Where is my third M going to be? Clearly, it has to be 2 or 3, otherwise I'll have 3 S's in a row (2-3-4). So 6 and 7 are S (the only M I have left will be either 2 or 3):

1	2	3	4	5	6	7
M			S	M	S	S

The best try to make this work is to use 2 for the third M (otherwise I'm alternating M-S-M-S-M...no way will that work). So...does it work?

1	2	3	4	5	6	7
M	M	S	S	M	S	S

Three cleanings...it COULD be true that the 4th load is stone, so **Answer Choice (B) is correct.** Let's prove that the other choices are wrong:

(C) Starting point:

1	2	3	4	5	6	7
M	S	M	S	M	S	S

Remember, I'm importing 1=M from (A) – once I know the first load can't be stone, it's mulch. So when I test answer choice (C), which asks if 3 can also be Mulch, I have a complete layout – M at 1, 3, and 5. This has five cleanings, so Answer Choice (C) is incorrect. And therefore, I now know that the third load has to be stone, so I can import that into my starting points for (D) and (E).

(D) Starting point:

1	2	3	4	5	6	7
M	S	S	S	M	M	S

Another choice that gives me the third M, thus a complete layout; it's just a matter of seeing if a rule is violated. The initial rules are ok, but question 17 says no more than two loads of the same material in a row – having S at 2, 3, and 4 violates that, so (D) is incorrect. I don't have a *rule* that 1 has to be M; I just know from (A) that if 1 *isn't* M, then the layout won't work, so I don't have to worry about it. For instance, switch the M at 1 here with the S at either 2 or 3, and you'll find that you need four cleanings. That won't work.

(E) Starting point:

1	2	3	4	5	6	7
M	S	S	S	M	S	M

This leaves 3 S's in a row, so it won't work. Answer choice (E) is incorrect.

GAME 4

Another great setup for my favorite "Grid Diagram": I have two known variables – the story location and the field – and one thing to figure out: Who's going to be where? That means my main diagram will look like this:

	R	S	T
P			
W			

R, S, and T are the locations, and P and W are the fields (Photographer/Writer). As I learn information about the interns, I'll drop them into the appropriate box. The checklist looks like this:

G & L = Same Field

F & K = Different Field

H = P

J = T

K ≠ S

One of these rules is extremely important in a very subtle way– the rule that F and K will be in different fields. Do you see how that will affect the game? The surprising (?) answer is, the rule fills up *both* groups! This is a key concept in grouping games. We know that G & L are in the same field; who will the third person in that field be? It will have to be either F or K, because one of them is in each field.

This in turn means that H & J are ALSO in the same field as each other (the one that G & L *aren't* in). There's no room in G & L's field for H *or* J, because F or K has to be in there, too, taking up the third and final spot. So it's G & L in one field, and H & J the other, with F & K split up. *And* we know that H is a Photographer. So J is also a photographer, and G and L are Writers. Reread these two paragraphs. Seriously.

Again, just to be sure you're ok on the reasoning: H is a Photographer (given). Can G also be a Photographer? No, because if G is, then so is L, and we'd be up to 3 Photographers PLUS either F or K, since one of them must be a Photographer.

Revised checklist:

G & L = W

H & J = P

F & K = Different Field

K ≠ S

Now that I know that J is a Photographer, and because I already knew that he was in Tuscany, I can take him out of my checklist and put him in my diagram (in parenthesis, since it's a permanent feature of this game):

	R	S	T
P			(J)
W			

These rules that two people are in different groups are very common, and this is pretty much always the purpose they serve – filling up the groups.

18. Again, this typical "first question" is just a matter of taking each answer choice and going down the checklist once (and making a good checklist and paying attention).

- (A) **Answer Choice (A) is correct.** I have 5 rules; (A) doesn't violate any of them. I love it when it's (A); I'm not even going to look at (B) through (E) – I'm on to question 19. Do your timed practice like that; it will improve your confidence (or drive the importance of making good diagrams and checklists into your mind).

- (B) Violates the rule that G and L will be trained in the same field (I've deduced that they're both going to be Writers, but even if I hadn't figured that out, from the initial rules I was given, I know that I can't have G without L or L without G).

- (C) Violates the rule that F and K will be trained in different fields – So one of them has to be a Photographer; here, they're both Writer's Assistants.

- (D) Violates the rule that H will be a Photographer. Be careful; just because you don't see H, you can't just zip past the rule that you have *about* H. This is a list of Photographers, so we need to see H on it.

- (E) Violates the rule that K is not assigned to Spain.

These "first questions" are fast, free points…but you can't afford to be sloppy.

19. It's a "Must Be True" question, so I'm going to take the given information for the *question* as true, then assume the given information for the *answer choice* is false, and see which one I can't eliminate.

(A) Because I'm trying to falsify the answer choice, I have to put G somewhere *other than Spain*. F has to be in Romania, but he can have either job. I'll try G in Tuscany with J, and I'll make F a writer, and see what happens. If that doesn't work, I'll try something else; I'm just trying to find a single layout that works. My initial assumptions give me this as a starting point:

	R	S	T
P			(J)
W	F		G

K can't be in Spain, so I have to make him a Photographer in Romania. Hall is also a Photographer, so that leaves L as a writer in Spain:

	R	S	T
P	K	H	(J)
W	F	L	G

That layout seems to work, which means that G does *not* have to be assigned to Spain, and (A) is incorrect.

(B) For this one, I have to take H out of Spain. Here's the systematic way to come up with a layout: Because (B) gives me additional information about H, I look to my checklist for H. H is a photographer; therefore, because J is the photographer in Tuscany, that means I have to put H in Romania (the only other 'non-Spain') with F. That makes F a writer (since H has to be a photographer). Now I'm up to:

	R	S	T
P	H		(J)
W	F		

Since I just learned something definite about F, I look to my rule about F and see that F has to be in a different field than K. That means that because F is a Writer, K must be a Photographer. But the only place left to be a Photographer is Spain, and K cannot be assigned to Spain. So, starting from the premise that H is not assigned to Spain, I've hit an unavoidable contradiction, which means that my assumption that H is not assigned to Spain was wrong. Since it *Cannot Be False* that H is assigned to Spain, it Must Be True, and **Answer Choice (B) is correct.** This is a very useful answer choice to work through a few times, particularly coming back to it fresh a couple of days after the first time you see it. It illustrates a very practical process. Again, on the actual LSAT, I wouldn't look at (C) through (E). I'd be on to question 20. But for the sake of completeness:

(C) The starting point is that K is *not* in Tuscany, and I already knew that he wasn't in Spain. That puts K in Romania with F. That will satisfy the requirement that F and K are in different fields. So H is the other Photographer, and I can divvy up G and L between Spain and Tuscany. One of a few possibilities is:

	R	S	T
P	K	H	(J)
W	F	G	L

This layout does not violate any rules, so K does *not* have to be assigned to Tuscany, and Answer Choice (C) is incorrect.

(D) Always be lazy when you can – the diagram I just created to analyze Answer Choice (C) also serves to eliminate (D); we've just shown that L can be in Tuscany, so he does not need to be in Spain. Answer Choice (D) is incorrect.

(E) Similarly, the layout that worked to disprove Answer Choice (A) also eliminates (E) – L does not have to be in Tuscany; he can be in Spain:

	R	S	T
P	K	H	(J)
W	F	L	G

So Answer Choice (E) is also incorrect. If I'd had to create this diagram from scratch, I'd start with L. I'm trying to put him out of Tuscany, so I try to drop him in Spain. L and G are both writers, so why not let G be the Writer in Tuscany, if L can't? That leaves F or K to be the Writer in Romania, so, say I go with F. Now I'm up to:

	R	S	T
P			(J)
W	F	L	G

Since I have to keep K out of Spain, that puts K in Romania and H in Spain, and there it is – a diagram that doesn't violate any rules and shows that L can be in Spain... so he doesn't have to be in Tuscany, and Answer Choice (E) is incorrect.

20. The question gives me information about F and H, so I check my rules about F & H. H is a Photographer, so if they're on the same story, F is a Writer. F and K are in different fields, so K is a Photographer. The Writers are G, L, and F, and the photographers are H, J, and K. It's a Could Be True question, so I'll just plug in the information from the answer choices, and the first one that works is the right answer.

(A) No need for a starting point here. F can't be in Tuscany, because J is in Tuscany, and that means F would be with J, but Question 20 requires that F be with H. So Answer Choice (A) is incorrect.

(B) Starting point:

	R	S	T
P			(J)
W	G		

F and H are supposed to be together, and that can only happen in Spain, so:

	R	S	T
P		H	(J)
W	G	F	

That leaves K in Romania and L in Tuscany. That layout doesn't violate any rules, so **Answer Choice (B) is correct.** By now you know that I wouldn't look at (C), (D), or (E), but let's do it anyway:

(C) Starting point:

	R	S	T
P	H		(J)
W	F		

The only remaining place for a Photographer is Spain, and K has to be a Photographer for this question, since he's not in the same field as F. But K can't be assigned to Spain, so Answer Choice (C) is incorrect.

(D) This one isn't worth a starting point diagram; I know that K has to be a Photographer (again, for this question only), but K cannot be the Photographer in Tuscany, because J is. So Answer Choice (D) is incorrect.

(E) Starting point:

	R	S	T
P			(J)
W		L	

F and H have to be together; there's only room for that to happen in Romania. Much like (C), above, though, that leaves only Spain for K, and K can't be assigned to Spain. So Answer Choice (E) is incorrect.

21. I start with F is a Writer, then I look to my rule about F and see that K must be a Photographer. So the Writers are G, L, and F; the Photographers are H, J, and K. It's a could be true question, so it should be easy enough to work through the answer choices.

(A) This choice is incorrect at a glance, because F and G are both writers; therefore, they can't work on the same story.

(B) This one shows one of the dangers of doing too much in your head. If you noticed that G and H are in different fields, and that each is permitted to be in Romania, then you might mark this answer choice as correct...and it would cost you a point. Get it on paper, and try to create an *entire* layout that satisfies the rules. If you do, here's what you'll find:

	R	S	T
P	H		(J)
W	G		

Oops...The only other spot for our last photographer (K) is Spain, and that can't happen. So (B) is incorrect. More importantly, if I didn't see it before, now I see that the photographers have to be in this order:

	R	S	T
P	K	H	(J)
W			

We've known all along that J is in Tuscany, so since K is a Photographer, K must be in Romania, leaving H in Spain. That should make the other answer choices easy to evaluate. (Did you notice that the Photographers had to be in this order for question 20, as well?)

(C) This is like (A); H and K are both Photographers, so they can't both be in Romania.

(D) This is the one that can work. I know K has to be in Romania, and I don't have any rules saying that the writers have to be anywhere in particular. One valid layout:

	R	S	T
P	K	H	(J)
W	L	F	G

So K and L can be in Romania, and **Answer Choice (D) is correct.**

(E) The same analysis as in Answer Choice (B) applies here; H cannot be in Romania, because that would force K to Spain, which violates an initial rule.

22. G and K are on the same story. Since the question gives me information about G and K, I check my rules about G and K. G is a Writer, so K is a Photographer. And since K is a Photographer, F is a Writer. So the Writers are F, G, and L; the Photographers are H, J, and K. G and K can't be in Spain (since K won't be assigned there), and they can't be in Tuscany (since J has a permanent assignment there). So my starting point is:

	R	S	T
P	K	H	(J)
W	G		

(A) is incorrect, because K and G are the ones in Romania.

(B) is incorrect, because G is in Romania, not Spain.

(C) is incorrect, because K and G are the ones in Romania.

(D) is incorrect, because K is in Romania, not Spain.

(E) **is correct.** Spain (like Tuscany) is a possibility for L.

23. The question is about Tuscany, so I check for rules about Tuscany, and I see that I have one – J is in Tuscany. Since I know that J is a Photographer, then I know that

anyone who is also a Photographer will not be able to go to Tuscany. The only Photographer for sure, besides J, is H, so **Answer Choice (C) is correct.**

If I did not make that connection, I would run down the answer choices one by one, assuming that each is true (again, it's a "Must Be False" question, so I try to *disprove* the answer choices by seeing if they Could Be True). Since J is a Photographer, I'll plug in each answer choice as a Writer in Tuscany. Here's how that would look:

(A) Starting point:

	R	S	T
P			(J)
W			F

The answer choice gives me information about F, so I look to my rule about F and see that F and K are in different fields. So K is a photographer. Since I learned something about K, I look to my rule about K and see that K is not in Spain, so K is in Romania. H is the other Photographer, so H gets Spain and I'm up to:

	R	S	T
P	K	H	(J)
W			F

There's no reason I can't put G and L down in the other two spots without violating any rules, so F CAN be assigned to Tusancy, and Answer Choice (A) is incorrect.

(B) I don't have any rules against just keeping the Photographers from the last layout...in that layout, G was a Writer anyway; what if I keep the top row the same, and switch G in for F. Then I could have something like:

	R	S	T
P	K	H	(J)
W	F	L	G

That seems to work just fine. So G CAN be assigned to Tuscany, and Answer Choice (B) is incorrect.

(C) If I put H in Tuscany, I go to my rules about H and see that H has to be a photographer. But J is my photographer in Tuscany, so clearly, H CANNOT be assigned to Tuscany, and **Answer Choice (C) is Correct**.

(D) Putting K in Tuscany gives me:

	R	S	T
P			(J)
W			K

This is different than the last couple of layouts, but I don't have a rule that says K can't be a Writer; K just has to be in a different field than F, and not in Spain. G and L are writers, so if I fill them in, along with F and H on the top:

	R	S	T
P	F	H	J
W	G	L	K

A quick scan of the checklist shows that I'm not violating any rules, so K CAN be assigned to Tuscany, and Answer Choice (D) is incorrect.

(E) The simplest thing is to just keep the top and bottom rows the same, if possible. I can't put K in Spain, but I can put K in Romania and bump everybody else one spot to the right, giving me:

	R	S	T
P	F	H	J
W	K	G	L

This layout shows that L *can* be in Tuscany, so Answer Choice (E) is incorrect.

Section 3 (Logical Reasoning)

1. Forethoughts: The first step in resolving (i.e. explaining) a discrepancy[18] is identifying it. Here, the discrepancy is pretty easy to spot – steps were taken to reduce congestion, but the result was that congestion *increased*. As always, I'm going to at least try to predict an answer, and in this case, one leaps right to mind – maybe with the improvements, everyone thinks traffic will be better, so a lot more people use those highways, creating congestion despite the improvements. This idea seems so obvious, I'd be surprised if it weren't an answer choice. Of course, I've been surprised before.

- (A) Correct. Exactly what I was looking for. I pretty much never move onto the next question in a Logical Reasoning section without looking at all of the answer choices, but if I were ever going to, this would be the question. How could this answer possibly be incorrect?

- (B) Incorrect. This answer choice sounds good, but notice that it states that projects typically start *after* the population has increased. If the population *already* increased before the project started, that doesn't explain why the project didn't decrease the problem. Contrast with (A), which explains why the project itself *contributes* to the problem.

- (C) Incorrect. This answer choice cuts the wrong way. If adding lanes *reduces* the rate of accidents, then traffic congestion should actually be even *less* of a problem. The passage tells us, though, that adding lanes makes traffic congestion *worse*. That doesn't explain the discrepancy; it makes it even more confusing.

- (D) This is the kind of sneaky thing the LSAT does to trick you. This shouldn't really an attractive answer choice, but if you found it to be one, I can understand. It's a good example of a distractor. You can read it and say, "Is there anything about urban areas in the passage?" Then you look up at the passage, and sure enough, they're talking about studies in urban areas, then you decide it makes sense to explain the traffic, and the next thing you know, you're missing a question. The reason it's a bad answer is that *it explains the wrong thing*. (D) discusses the difference between rural and urban areas, but that's not the point of the passage at all; the point of the passage is the difference between traffic *before* and *after* the highway widening. That's what we need to see in an answer choice.

---

[18] A "discrepancy" is just a couple of facts that seem at first to be inconsistent – it doesn't make sense that all of the facts are true. The right answer is the one that will make it makes sense. For instance, if I have a minimum wage job, but I drive a very expensive car, that's something of a discrepancy. It could be explained in a few ways – maybe the car was the only thing I inherited from my rich uncle. Or maybe I'm rich, but I keep my minimum wage job because I find it very rewarding. That's the sort of thing we're looking for – the explanation that's going to make it all make sense.

(E) Exactly the same analysis as in (D), above. Don't get tricked into thinking about why urban or rural areas might have more traffic. That whole comparison is beside the point. It's not about rural vs. urban; it's about before highways get widened vs. after they get widened.

Afterthoughts: It's easier to avoid distractor answers if you make a prediction. Also, always keep in mind the relevant comparisons. Also, if an answer choice is off-point, even if it seems "true," it's wrong. (D) and (E) compare rural to urban areas, not 'before' and 'after' a highway is widened. Remember, for the purposes of this question, we're assuming *each* of the answer choices (in turn) is true. We're not looking for "the true" answer choice; we're looking for the one that explains a specific point.

As far as predicting correct answer goes, it's like the difference between going shopping with a list, and going grocery shopping when you're hungry. If you know what you're looking for, you're probably going to find it, buy it, and get on with your life. If you just walk up and down the aisles at random, you're going to spend a lot of time there, and you're probably not going to get what you want. Try to know what you're looking for.

2. Forethoughts: Kind of hard to come up with a predicted answer on this one. Who knows what they might come up with to strengthen the argument? One thing I always have in mind, though, on strengthen/weaken questions, is the idea of the alternative explanation. What's happening is, after the advertisement, people are buying the product. The conclusion is that the advertisement is working. It's *possible*, though, that more people are buying the product for another reason. A good "strengthen" answer choice is often one that *negates* a possible alternative explanation.

(A) This answer choice does not strengthen the argument. The premises show that people are more *likely to buy the product* after the advertisement. Even if the advertisement somehow drives people to race to the checkout and make purchases, that doesn't tell us that those people are more likely to buy the product. We're not looking for more people going through the checkout line; we're looking for a higher likelihood of people buying the product. (A) doesn't strengthen the argument, because it doesn't tell us anything about how likely the shoppers are to buy the product.

(B) Correct. This is exactly what I mean by "negating a possible alternative explanation." The evidence is that a lot of people bought the product after hearing it advertised; one possibility is that maybe it's a coincidence – those people were going to buy that product anyway. This answer choice, if true, *eliminates* that possibility; that strengthens the argument's conclusion – that the increase in sales is due to the advertisement.

(C) This answer choice might sound kind of good at first, but it's really not saying much of anything. First, the word "many" is extremely vague, logically speaking. Moreover, it doesn't give us anything to use to distinguish between the comparison groups, because "many of the consumers" doesn't tell us how many of them were in the group who got to the checkout line *before* hearing the ad and how many got to the checkout line *after* hearing it. If the group who went to the checkout line *after* hearing the ad "typically" buys the advertised product, that would actually weaken the conclusion, because then we'd have a reason to think that they didn't buy it because of the ad – they bought it because that's what they always do. Contrast with (B), which tells us specifically about the consumers *who bought the advertised product*. They *weren't* planning to buy it, then they hear the advertisement, then they *do* buy it. The scenario in (B) sounds much more like the advertisement itself was the reason for the purchase.

(D) This probably neither strengthens nor weakens the argument. "Subliminal" advertising is pretty much common knowledge by now; the ad could have affected them without their remembering it. If you don't know about subliminal advertising, you'd probably think an ad only works if the customer hears it. But if *that* were true, (D) would *weaken* the argument. If a consumer has to be consciously aware of an advertisement for it to be effective, and if the consumer *wasn't* consciously aware of it, then the conclusion that the advertisements are effective is weakened – the consumer must have bought the product for another reason. The better interpretation, though, is that the ad works or doesn't work regardless of whether the customer active hears it, or remembers hearing it, so the additional information that (D) provides is just meaningless.

(E) Buying a product "only occasionally" is not directly related to the conclusion that the advertisements are effective, because we don't know if those "occasions" coincide with the advertisements. If "only occasionally" means "only when they're advertised," the argument would be strengthened, but (E) doesn't say that, so we can't draw a meaningful conclusion from (E) either way, even if we assume it's true. So (E) is irrelevant.

Afterthoughts: This question (and (B) in particular) provides another good example of the "alternative explanation" in action. It's an extremely common theme on the LSAT. Look for it often, but especially on Strengthen (or Weaken) the Argument questions, or on "Find the Flaw" questions.

3. Forethoughts: I'll talk about "unless" in the Afterthoughts. It gives students a lot of problems. The first premise is that one of two things needs to happen to get the library open on schedule – getting the building permit by February 1, or finishing some of the other necessary activities faster than planned. We're also told that the building permit

will not be obtained by February 1; that means the only chance to get the library completed on schedule is finishing those "other activities" faster than planned. And since the conclusion is that the library WON'T be completed on schedule, then the unstated premise (assumption) is probably just going to be that those other activities won't be finished faster than had been originally planned.

- (A) Correct. If this unstated premise is added to the passage, then we have: "1 of 2 things needs to happen to finish the library on schedule. The first thing isn't going to happen (permit), and the second thing isn't going to happen, either (early completion of the other activities – answer choice (A)). Therefore, the library won't finish on schedule." Perfectly valid.

- (B) This answer choice can't help the conclusion follow "logically from the premises," because it pretty much ignores the premises entirely. Moreover, it says that the library "probably" won't be completed on schedule; the passage's conclusion is that it (definitely) won't be. Additionally, note that the passage is about what consequences will follow from what preconditions – obtaining the permit and completing other activities. Whether or not anything gets "admitted" doesn't address those preconditions. Besides, maybe the officials are just wrong. There are many reasons this is not a good answer choice.

- (C) All this answer choice does is confirm what we're already told in the passage – the building permit will not be obtained by February 1. That's still not enough to get us to the conclusion, because it doesn't account for the other possibility – that some of those "other activities" may be completed faster than originally thought.

- (D) This is essentially (C) all over again – it tells us why the building permit won't be obtained in time. We really don't care *why* we won't have the building permit. As far as the argument is concerned, it only matters whether or not we'll actually have the permit by February 1. The passage already tells us we won't, so this answer choice doesn't add anything new. The *reason* we won't have the permit (need to revise the building plan) doesn't matter at all.

- (E) This one is a little sneakier. The passage doesn't tell us that we need to begin construction before the permit is obtained, so this is a red herring[19]. For instance, if we obtained the permit on February 1, for all we know from the passage, we could start construction months later and still complete the project on time. The passage doesn't say when we need to start construction; only when we obtain the permit. Additionally, to reach the passage's conclusion, we need to negate *both* possibilities – the permit, and also the completion of those "other

---

[19] Red herring: "A piece of information intended to be misleading or distracting from the actual issue."

activities." From the passage, we had already given up on the permit idea; we're really looking for an answer choice that eliminates the second option.

Afterthoughts: "Unless" gives a lot of students problems. Let's say there was only one condition in the passage – "Unless the permit is obtained by Feb. 1, the library won't be finished on time." That statement is often misread to say, "*If* the permit is obtained by Feb. 1, the library *will* be finished on time." That formulation is incorrect. The actual meaning of the statement, in pure conditional terms (If-Then) is, "If the permit *is not* obtained by Feb. 1, the library *will not* be finished on time." In other words, obtaining the permit by Feb. 1 is a *necessary* condition for finishing the library on time, but not a *sufficient* one.

Let's look at it another way; let's say a glass of beer costs $4. "Unless Joe has $4, you cannot buy a glass of beer." Does that mean "If Joe has $4, he can buy a glass of beer"? No! What if Joe is 14 years old? Then he can't buy the beer even if he has the money. What the original statement means is, "If Joe *doesn't* have $4, he *cannot* buy a glass of beer." Properly getting rid of words like "unless" is important, because you want to be able to see the statement in If-Then terms in order to ascertain the contrapositive.

Ok, that's the explanation; how about a simple rule, instead? Leave the "then" part of the sentence alone, but change the "If" to "If NOT." Let's look at the passage, but pretend only the permit mattered. We'd have "Unless the permit is obtained by Feb. 1, the library won't be built in time." Even though there's not "then" written into the sentence, the "then part" is the *consequence*. It's the second underlined part – everything after the comma. So we're going to replace "unless" with "if," but also *negate* the first part of the sentence, and leave the second part alone: "IF the permit IS NOT obtained by Feb. 1, the library won't be built in time."

Back to the complete passage – Here, there are *two* possible ways to get the library built on time. We're told that one of them (Permit by Feb. 1) isn't happening. Because the conclusion tells us that the library is definitely not going to be built on time, we need to know that the *other* possibility (completing some of those other activities in less time than was originally planned) isn't going to come through, either. If this second possibility weren't negated, we couldn't conclude that the opening would be delayed; we'd be able to say, "Well, maybe they can complete some of those other activities faster than they thought." That's the hope the passage gives us. (A) kills that possibility.

4. Forethoughts: Again, Weaken (or Strengthen) the Argument questions are almost always good candidates to be on the lookout for an alternative explanation. Reading over the question, it seems to be a cinch that's what's going on here. The premises are that the people who sniffed peppermint had a harder time falling asleep than those who sniffed orange, and orange doesn't help you fall asleep, so the peppermint must have made it worse. I'm looking for an alternative explanation – in other words, a reason

(other than peppermint causes insomnia) that explains why the peppermint group might have had a harder time falling asleep.

- (A) The passage gives us information on what happens when people who DO have insomnia inhale peppermint. The conclusion is not about people who *don't* have insomnia and inhale peppermint. This answer choice won't affect the conclusion, because it pertains to a different group of people – those *without* insomnia.

- (B) Correct. Exactly what I'm looking for – an alternative explanation as to why the group that inhaled peppermint had a harder time falling asleep than the ones who inhaled bitter orange. The reason was that the "orange group" had milder cases of insomnia. So the "peppermint group" didn't have a harder time falling asleep *because peppermint makes insomnia worse* (the conclusion of the passage); they had a harder time falling asleep because they had worse insomnia in the first place.

- (C) Knowing that they were involved in a study doesn't suggest why the peppermint group wouldn't fall asleep as easy as the orange group. If knowing you're in a study makes it harder to fall asleep, why didn't the "orange group" fall asleep slower? Or if it knowing they were in a study made it easier for the "orange group," why didn't the "peppermint group" fall asleep easier, too? It's not about how easy or hard it is to fall asleep *in general*; we need something that will distinguish between the two groups –a reason that applies to the "peppermint group" but not the "orange group." The conclusion is about one of the two groups (peppermint group) but not the other, so an answer choice that doesn't separate the groups won't get us there. This is common – Many answer choices are wrong because the ignore the comparison that is central to the argument.

- (D) Many problems with such a short answer choice. The passage is about "difficulty *falling* asleep," not *staying* asleep. Furthermore, even if difficulty staying asleep is a measure of insomnia, (D) (like (C)) does nothing to distinguish between the two groups. Finally, "some people" could be just a single person[20]; that's not enough to have much of an impact on the conclusion. "Some people" who smoke live to be 100 years old; does that shake your belief that smoking is bad for you?

- (E) This tells us nothing important. It might strengthen the argument, for all we know – maybe peppermint is one of those "certain pleasant scents" that can affect the degree to which a patient suffers from insomnia – by making it worse! Really, though, it's irrelevant. We don't have any information about which scents

---

[20] On the LSAT, "some" means "more than none" – that is, at least one. "Some" is not necessarily plural (as it is in casual conversation), and it could even be "all."

(E) is referring to. On top of that, we aren't told whether those scents make insomnia better or worse. (E) is really too vague to be much use.

Afterthoughts: I hope you're starting to see why I belabor the "alternative explanation" idea. It shows up *all the time* on the LSAT. That's one reason I'm not a big fan of the obsession to categorize everything in terms of "question types." It's about the structure of the *argument*, not the question; if you understand how a possible alternative explanation relates to an argument, you'll be able to find it whether the question itself is framed as Strengthen, Weaken, Find the Flaw, Find the Assumption, etc.

5. Forethoughts: The prompt lets me know ahead of time that I'm trying to find the function of one particular part of the passage. Reading the passage, it seems pretty clear that it's the main (actually, the only) conclusion. It doesn't support any other statements, and the statement that comes next supports it (apart from the content, the phrase "After all" suggests that support is on the way for something that's already been said; it's a premise indicator). In other words, we have a two-sentence argument – a conclusion, followed (and supported) by a premise.

   (A) The key phrase is not a premise. Premises act in support of conclusions. The statement isn't being in used to support any other statement; instead, it is the statement *being* supported. Since it isn't a premise, it isn't an "explicit" premise.

   (B) First and foremost, it's not "implicit." As the word suggests, "implicit" means *implied*. The sentence was plainly stated, which makes it *explicit* – the opposite of implicit. It's also not an assumption; the writer doesn't just *assume* it to be true – he supports it with the second sentence.

   (C) It isn't "background" information; it's the main point. It does not "help facilitate understanding" the issue; it IS the issue. The sentence in question is the whole ball of wax – the claim that either you buy into based on the premise offered in support, or you reject. There's no background involved.

   (D) Correct. This one stops me in my tracks a little, because I've identified the key statement as a conclusion, and the word "conclusion" does not appear in this answer choice. However, it IS a statement, and the argument DOES claim that the study supports it. That claim of support is based on the phrase "after all," which indicates a link between the two sentences.

   (E) Sneaky, sneaky. I've eliminated (A), (B), and (C), and I'm a little taken aback that (D) didn't mention a "conclusion," and now here is an answer choice that *does* identify the statement as a conclusion! But in no way is it an "intermediate" conclusion (a conclusion that is then used as a premise for another, more important, conclusion). What main conclusion could the sentence possibly be "in direct support" of? This is a one-conclusion passage. Maybe if they dressed it up with a longer paragraph, I might be tempted to stray, but there are only two sentences here. I don't have multiple conclusions.

Afterthoughts: Whenever you have these questions that ask you in general terms about a portion of a passage, take those general terms in the answer choices, and try to match them up to content-specific portions of the passage. For instance, as I'm looking at (D), what do I see? It's a statement – check! The argument claims it's supported by the study – check! On the other hand, look at (E): "...support for the argument's main conclusion"?! That's not going to work, because there's no other sentence in the passage that I could describe as being "the argument's main conclusion." Here's an example of an argument with an intermediate conclusion:

John would be a good leader. After all, smart people make good leaders, and clearly John is smart, since he went to Harvard.

The intermediate (or "subsidiary") conclusion is that John is smart – it's a conclusion, because it's based on the premise that he went to Harvard and the assumption (implied premise) that people who go to Harvard are smart. But it's not the final resting point of the argument; once we conclude that John is smart, we turn that observation into a premise by combining it with the premise that smart people make good leaders, and that gets us to the *main* conclusion – that John would be a good leader. We know it's the main conclusion, because the argument stops there – everything else supports the statement that he would be a good leader.

6. Forethoughts: To find the most similar reasoning among the answer choices, I'm first going to restate the reasoning of the passage in general terms, in a simplified way that I can easily understand. In this case, that's not too hard – it's a very straightforward argument. X (difficulty) has not been true for a bunch of people who have previously done something (flown the plane), so it probably won't be true for the next person.

(A) Reading over this choice, I see that I may have oversimplified my translation of the passage – the conclusion of the answer choice is about the "average reader," but the premise is about book reviewers – people with some expertise. In the passage, the conclusion and the premise were both about people some expertise – test pilots. A conclusion that switches groups like that is less reliable that one that is consistent. In other words, what's true for pilots is true for pilots, but what's true for book reviewers *isn't* necessarily true for "average readers." Maybe I'll get back to this one, but it looks like an important difference.

(B) This one I can clearly eliminate. Why? Because it's similar to (A), but worse. It makes the same (potential) error that (A) makes – shifting from book reviewers to "people" (sounds about like "average readers"), but it also makes another one –

it relies on the opinion of "*most* of the book reviewers." The passage, like answer choice (A), relies on a unanimous sample. So even if the shift from reviewers to average readers is acceptable, (A) will still be better than (B).

(C) This choice is consistent about referencing "reviewers," but the fact that we're relying on only two reviewers is suspect. That sure doesn't sound like "many[21]." So far, I'm just seeing answer choices that are consistent with the logic of the passage (the person in the conclusion will do what the people in the premise did), but somehow they're all falling a little short. At this point, I'm just hoping to get to an answer choice that's right on point. If it doesn't happen, then I'll have to worry about sorting out which is the best of the imperfect options.

(D) Correct. This is pretty much exactly what I was hoping for. We have the same "number" of people in the premise of the answer choice as the passage (many), and we're staying consistent with "reviewers." Finally, a real match.

(E) By now, this should sound a lot like (A) (and (B)) – we've gone from "reviewers" to "the general public." That doesn't necessarily make it a horrible parallel, but when we have an alternative, (D), that *doesn't* make that shift, then (E) isn't going to be the "most similar" to the passage.

Afterthoughts: The gist of an argument is that leap from premise(s) to conclusion – from what we know (here, what has already happened) to what we expect (here, what will happen). When you see shifts in the terms, take note of them. The passage starts *and* finishes by talking about pilots. Many of the wrong answer choices shift from "reviewers" to...something else (average readers, general public, whatever). Don't let those seemingly small changes go unnoticed. They're usually important.

7. Forethoughts: Since I'm being referred to a specific term in the argument, I'm going to start at that term and work backward. Astrology is mentioned as an illustration of something, clearly; it is introduced by the phrase "to see this," which indicates that it's an example of a larger point, and that larger point is going to be found in the immediately preceding sentence. That preceding sentence also has a "this" in it, so I'm going back to the first sentence. If this seems tedious and/or difficult, by the way, get used to it – welcome to the study and practice of law. Bill Clinton is a smart guy; there's a reason he asked what the definition of "is" is.

The second sentence's "this" is referring to something that affects our perception of the world, from the first sentence. According to the second sentence, affecting our

---

[21] By the way, watch out for "many"; it's just too vague. On the LSAT, "some" means "at least one." "Most" means "more than half." "All" means, well, "all." But "many"? If you find out what, exactly, that one means, let me know. Doesn't mean it's always a wrong answer; for instance, if the premise is "many," that would support a conclusion of "some" (at least one). But it's imprecise in a way that should provoke your distrust.

perception of the world is not enough for a theory to be taken seriously. Going back to the final sentence, then, astrology is an example illustrating the second sentence – in other words, it's an example of something that affects our perception of the world, but shouldn't necessarily be taken seriously.

- (A) The idea that a theory that DOESN'T affect our world SHOULDN'T be taken seriously is the contrapositive of the *first* sentence; Astrology is being used to illustrate the *second* sentence, which has a different key idea – that even if an idea affects our perception of the world, that STILL might not be enough to take it seriously.

- (B) The passage doesn't offer any criteria for disqualifying something as a theory. The issues are whether or not a theory affects our perception of the world, and if so, whether or not that theory should be taken seriously. This is a good example of an answer choice that is incorrect because it is outside the scope of the passage.

- (C) Correct. This is what the scientist is getting at. Affecting our perception of the world is not enough for a theory to be taken seriously – for astrology to be a useful example of his point, it has to be a theory that (1) DOES affect our perception of the world, but (2) nevertheless should NOT be taken seriously.

- (D) No. The "astrology sentence" refers us directly to the second sentence, which states explicitly that affecting our perception of the world "is *not*, in itself, enough for a theory to be taken seriously."

- (E) This is the poorest of the answer choices, as it directly contradicts the first sentence. The scientist states that a theory that is to be taken seriously MUST affect our perception of the world; he is not bringing up an example to illustrate that the first thing he said was incorrect.

Afterthoughts: I wasn't being flippant…there's a BUNCH of parsing of language to do in legal practice (and maybe even more in law school). Figuring out which words pronouns refer to, deleting an optional comma, reading "closed" as an adverb vs. a verb…these are all examples I remember very well from analyzing cases and statutes, and they can all affect the outcome of a case. Of course, in law school and in the practice of law, you'll have more than a minute and a half to make those determinations (a luxury you don't have in LSAT-land), but nevertheless…there's a lot of careful reading to do. Fortunately, this was a short passage. The moral of this story is, when you see pronouns in the passage (e.g. "this"), make sure you know what they refer to.

8. Forethoughts: That first sentence is pretty much just a little introduction to the topic. It's the second sentence that's the premise, and the final sentence is the conclusion. I'm looking for a flaw here, and it doesn't seem that difficult to spot – in the premise, critical

acclaim is given as "one of the main factors." That doesn't support a conclusion that it is *necessary* for the selection of a play. Maybe her play was so good that they used it even though she's *not* a critically acclaimed playwright. This one should be easy.

- (A) The "criteria" in the passage are criteria for a play's being selected, not criteria for being critically acclaimed. We have no idea whether there are any special conditions "necessary for a playwright's being critically acclaimed."

- (B) When you see very general answer choices like this one, always try to find the content-specific material in the passage that matches up to the general answer choice. For instance, what could the "several different effects" be that this answer choice is referencing to? It doesn't make sense to me.

- (C) Correct. This answer choice is a nice contrast to (B), above. Look in the passage, and you'll see a perfect match to the answer choice. Do we have "one main factor"? Yes, the passage tells us specifically that a critically acclaimed playwright is just that – one main factor. Does it treat that as a condition that "must be met" for selection? Yes, the passage concludes that because a particular play was selected, it *must* include that factor.

- (D) There is no reference to an unreliable source of evidence. The factual evidence comes from a statement made by Clark – Clark tells us everything we know about the selection of the play. Why would Clark be unreliable? It's not like the passage tells us that Clark smokes crack three times a day from a jail cell where he's doing time for perjury and fraud. This answer choice is baseless.

- (E) There's no evidence that acclaim is the result, rather than the cause, of selection because it's *not*. The passage tells us flat-out that it's the other way around. The playwright's acclaim is the cause of the selection, because it's one of the criteria for selection. This answer choice is just in there to try to confuse you. Mixing up cause and effect is a common flaw, and it does show up on the LSAT quite a bit, but it doesn't apply here.

Afterthoughts: This one is fairly straightforward, and illustrates a common flaw. Here's another of my famous analogies to illustrate: gas mileage might be "one of the main factors" I'm considering as I go out car shopping. But if I find a car that's on sale for a great price, looks fantastic, and is very safe, I might buy it even if it gets lousy mileage. Even though mileage was a main factor in the selection process, you couldn't conclude that because I bought Car X, it "must get good gas mileage." As for (E), remember, a true statement can be a wrong answer.

9. Forethoughts: Here I have what looks like most of a classical syllogism (e.g. "All men are mortal; Socrates is a man; therefore, Socrates is mortal"), except that the major

premise (the categorization, i.e. "All men are mortal") is missing. In other words, it's like a (sufficient) assumption question, in that there's a gap between the stated premise and the conclusion, and the theorist's assumption is going to connect that gap. The stated premise is that diaries are another form of talking to oneself. The conclusion is that diaries shouldn't be used against their writers in criminal case. The common thread is diaries; what's missing a link between talking to yourself and criminal prosecution. The (missing) major premise should look something like, "Comments that you make to yourself should not be used against you in a criminal case." That supports the argument – the premise fit diaries into the larger category of "comments to one's self", and the missing principle puts everything in the larger category into the still larger category of "things that should not be used in a criminal case."

- (A) This does not connect diaries to things the government should not be allowed to use, because diaries are not "interoffice memos." Also, it's hard to see how a corporate official is analogous to an individual keeping a diary. Moreover, there's a great deal of emphasis in the passage (indeed, the entire sole stated premise) about how a diary is *individual*, "keeping one's thoughts to oneself." The memos in this answer choice are directed to *other people* – from corporate officials to government investigators. (A) is a poor fit.

- (B) The passage isn't limited to "when crime is a serious problem;" this answer choice isn't going to get us to the larger conclusion that governments should be able to use them, period. Moreover, there's nothing in the passage about varying the amount of power that governments should have to conduct their investigations.

- (C) Correct. "Unless…intended for other people" means that when remarks are NOT intended for other people, they shouldn't be used. This bridges the gap between diaries, which are not intended for other people, and things that shouldn't be used in criminal prosecutions – the new term that shows up in the conclusion.

- (D) This is a better answer choice than (A) or (B), but the problem with it is that a diary *isn't* "personal correspondence." The passage actually makes this distinction clearly, in the mind of the theorist at the very least – keeping a diary is not different than keeping your thoughts *to yourself*, or talking *to yourself* – those things aren't "personal correspondence."

- (E) This answer choice does not support the theorist's argument in any way. It actually undercuts it – doing "everything in their power" would include using diaries as evidence. The theorist, on the other hand, is arguing that the government should *not* be allowed to do some things within their power.

Afterthoughts: While it's always helpful to identify the conclusion, once you've found it, don't neglect the premise(s). The premise in the passage really emphasizes the notion of a diary being an individual, personal thing – the words "one's" and "oneself" are used five times in a single sentence. This is a clear red flag –the missing principle almost has to recognize the distinction between thoughts/words intended for oneself, and those intended to be conveyed to others.

10. Forethoughts: Sometimes you get a question that you can't really get your brain around at first glance. Frankly, for me, this is one of those. I have no idea how the flickering per second, 49-kilometer radius, and spinning black hole are supposed to relate to each other. Here's what you do when that happens: Don't worry about it; just go to the answer choices and see if one of them makes sense.

- (A) The passage gives me a scenario that involves a ring with a radius of "as close as" 49 kilometers, but it doesn't suggest how it would change things if the radius were *more than* 49 kilometers. So it's off-scope. I can't infer anything about the inverse.[22]

- (B) The word "only" invokes the inverse; in other words, this answer choice is saying that "rings of gas that are NOT in stable orbits…do NOT emit flickering X-rays." The passage is telling us about *one* ring of gas – and it *is* in a stable orbit, but for all we know, other rings of gas (that might not be in stable orbits) could emit flickering X-rays, too. We just don't have any information either way.

- (C) Correct. This one gets off to a good start, because it talks about the specific black hole that we have some information about, not black holes in general. So we only have to decide whether we have enough information in the passage to conclude that it's spinning. From the last sentence, it would not maintain its close orbit if it were not ("unless it was") spinning. It *is* maintaining its orbit (the orbit is "stable"), so it must be spinning (that's the contrapositive).

- (D) No, no, no…a thousand times, no. One of the most common logical fallacies committed in the real world is to infer cause without a sufficient basis. The passage tells us absolutely nothing about *why* some black holes spin. It only tells us that *if* it isn't spinning, then the gas ring could not maintain its close orbit.

- (E) The answer choice says that the black hole stationary "only if" it has a ring of gas more than 49 miles in radius orbiting it. That means if it DOESN'T have a ring of

---

[22] The passage tells us what we can expect if the ring's radius is as close as 49 kilometers; we can't infer anything about if the ring ISN'T as close as 49 kilometers. From a conditional statement (If P, then Q), you can't infer anything about "If NOT P…(then not Q)" My favorite real life example of this comes from a restaurant bathroom – A sign says, "Employees should was their hands after using bathroom." As a conditional statement, that would read, "If you're an employee, then you should wash your hands…." Does that mean, "If you're NOT an employee, then you SHOULDN'T wash your hands"? I hope not!

gas more than 49 miles in radius, then it's NOT stationary (again, to get rid of the "only," we negate everything). The passage tells us that the ring of gas we know about doesn't have a ring of gas *more than* 49 miles (it's exactly 49 miles), and according to (E), that should mean it's not stationary (which it isn't; it's spinning); BUT, per the passage, it only has to be spinning if the ring is "so close" (as the one we know about).

It's getting a little convoluted, but all we know from the passage is that it has to be spinning *if the gas ring is so close*. A gas ring way out in the distance might be orbiting a stationary black hole (according to the passage). That doesn't justify (E), which makes a blanket statement about the size of the gas ring and ignores the fact that the passage only talks about spinning/stationary when the gas ring in question is close.

Afterthoughts: So that whole 49-kilometer thing was just a false trail all along. Who'd have thought?! I could have written this one up as if everything made perfect sense from the beginning, but honestly, this was one of those questions that after I read the passage, I was saying, "What the heck?!" And I wanted to write it up that way, because the reality is, you'll have that feeling when you read some questions, too. Hopefully, not too many. And you have to deal with those questions, and you have to do it somewhat quickly. What you *don't* want to do is turn into the deer in the headlights, stare at it for 2 minutes, and end up no closer than when you started. If the passage isn't too long, you'll probably want to reread it, but if you're still in the same position, then just let yourself be guided by the answer choices. If you feel like the passage isn't something you really understand, just let it be a reference guide, to "look up" the answer choices and see if support for them is found there. Finally, be sure you understand conditional statements that include some of the tricky wording – "unless" and "only if."

11. Forethoughts: Another necessary assumption question. My first instinct, as always, is to look for a term that shows up in the conclusion that doesn't appear in the premises. Here, it's "intensity." The main premise that links to the conclusion (linked by common reference to the past two centuries) is the death of the species of coral. The assumption must pertain to a link between wiping out the coral and the intensity of the black water phenomenon. This gets us back to my favorite weapon against Logical Reasoning questions – the alternative explanation idea. If I can think of a good alternative explanation – something *other than the intensity of the black water* – that might account for the destruction of the coral, then the assumption they're looking for might be that the alternative explanation ISN'T true.

Here's an analogy: Let's say I go to my friend's house, and my friend has never owned a dog, but when I get there, there's a dog in his house. My conclusion is that my friend got a dog. Can you think of another explanation for the fact that there's a dog in the house?

Maybe he's watching the neighbor's dog for a few days. So you could identify an *assumption* that I'm making (in assuming that my friend got his own dog) as, "The dog does *not* belong to his neighbor." I'm going to be on the lookout for similar reasoning here – the assumption may be that a *different* explanation for the dead coral isn't true.

- (A) Incorrect. The conclusion is that in the past two centuries, even if black water has struck, it has not struck the bay *with as much intensity* as last year. It's not <u>required</u> that there hasn't been any black water; it might come every single years – just not with this much intensity. Remember, it's a *necessary* assumption question.

- (B) Incorrect. The argument is relying on how much damage was done to *five particular* coral species. There's nothing that suggests that damage to "every species" is important to the argument. For all we know from the passage, there could be a number of other species that weren't seriously harmed.

- (C) Like (B), above, this answer choice tries to bring in other species that aren't necessary to the argument. The argument is based on the severity of the damage to five specific species of coral; it's not relying on damage to plants or animals that make use of the coral (just like in (B), it's not relying on any coral other than the five species). Also notice, by the way, this answer choice actually *hurts* the argument. It lessens the severity of the black water by pointing out life forms that it did *not* decimate. Doesn't that make it LESS likely, if anything, that it was the most intense black water phenomenon in the past 200 years?

- (D) Correct. Restating the argument in a simple sentence, it's something like, "Last year's black water was the most intense in 200 years, because it killed coral that had been around for more than 200 years." But the year in which the coral died is only a good measure of the strength of the black water if the coral was relatively healthy. If it HAD BEEN "especially fragile" last year, then the conclusion would be poor, because the coral might have died *because of that fragility*, not the strength of the black water. So the assumption is that it WASN'T especially fragile last year.

    Because this is a necessary assumption question, we can use the negation technique - If the coral *was* much stronger in the past, the conclusion falls apart – We don't know that last year's black watering was the most intense, because a more intense black water phenomenon might have come along 100 years ago, but it didn't wipe out the coral *because the coral was stronger then*. Assuming that answer choice is false confirms that (D) is the right answer – when you negate the correct answer choice, the conclusion falls apart, but only for *necessary* assumption question (which is why it's critical to distinguish between necessary and sufficient assumption questions).

(E) If anything, this actually hurts the argument. If older specimens are more vulnerable, then the coral that was wiped out would have been stronger 100 years ago (when they weren't as old), so there might have been a more intense phenomenon that didn't wipe out the coral only because the coral was stronger when it was younger. This is sort of like the opposite of the correct answer, (D). The correct assumption is that the coral was *not* especially fragile; this answer choice suggests that the coral *was* at its most fragile last year, because it was older than it had been in past years.

Afterthoughts: I think this is one of the harder problems in Section 3. It does serve as a useful example of how the "alternative explanation" approach can help. Also, the technique of negating the answer choices; if you negate (D) (i.e. the coral WERE in especially fragile condition), the argument falls apart.

If you were in a hurry on this question, or just weren't seeing it, there's another useful technique that could have helped you here. The evidence cited in the passage pertains to five specific species of coral. Look at the wrong answer choices: (A) doesn't mention the coral at all; (B) discusses "every species of coral," (C) talks about plants and animals, and (E) talks about "older and younger" species of coral. Only (D) talks specifically about the coral that was used to reach the conclusion in the passage. Not a coincidence.

12. Forethoughts: The statements in the passage relate in a few different ways. I'm going to go to the answer choices and evaluate each one in turn to see if it's justified, but I will pay particular attention to the last sentence of the passage, which gives me a definite conditional (If → Then) relationship.

(A) This one may seem superficially attractive, but it's easy to dismiss. "Most" has a specific meaning – more than half. That conclusion is not justified, because the passage tells us how "some" nurseries label some plants. "Some" means at least one; that could be exactly one nursery, or it could be all of them. The passage doesn't lead to a conclusion about "most" nurseries.

(B) This is the tricky one to sort out. The key to untangling it is the "only if" language. If they're not in the simplest format, you should always translate conditional statements into simple "If → Then" statements, and to do that, you need to get rid of terms like "unless" or "only if." The statement "Q, only if P"[23] means "If NOT P, then NOT Q." This is an important one to know, and might be hard to work out until you're used to it, because there's no negation in the sentence; the negation is implied by "only." For instance, the statement "You can be president of the USA only if you're at least 35 years old" doesn't really tell you

---

[23] Philosophers and philosophy students arbitrarily use "P" and "Q" for conditional logic, in the same way that mathematicians use "X" and "Y" for algebra (and other letters for other mathematical constructs).

anything about people who are 35 or over. If you meet a 40 year old, he might be eligible for president, or he might not[24]. What the sentence really means is, "If you're NOT at least 35 years old, then you CAN'T be president.

So this answer choice, which says, "Only if the variety is UNsuitable" means "If the variety is *suitable* (NOT unsuitable), then some of the nurseries have mislabeled (NOT 'correctly labeled) it." Is that statement justified by the passage? *No.* The passage's premise begins, "If a variety is NOT suitable…" We cannot infer from that anything about the inverse ("If a variety IS suitable…"). In generalized logic terms, you can't go from "If P, then Q" to "If NOT P…"

(C) We are not told anything that helps us to determine whether the Stark Sweet Melody nectarine trees are miniature or not. The passage doesn't tell us whether they're suitable for growing in a tub or pot. So we cannot determine whether or not it would be correct to label them "miniature."

(D) The passage only tells us when trees that *are* labeled miniature are incorrectly labeled. From that premise, we can't tell whether or not a tree that *isn't* labeled miniature is incorrectly labeled. Maybe the only mistakes occur when trees *are* labeled incorrectly.

(E) Correct. Another one that needs to be translated, because of the "unless." This answer choice, in If → Then terms, is, "If the SSM variety tree is NOT suitable etc. etc., then some nurseries mislabel it." That fits the passage – If it's not suitable, then it can't be correctly labeled "miniature," and the passage tells us that some nurseries DO label it miniature, so those nurseries mislabel it.

Afterthoughts: Another tough question, frankly (certainly under time constraints). The best way to tackle it is to untangle those conditional statements that contain the sneaky terms like "unless" and "only if." Otherwise, it's just too tricky trying to evaluate those sentences to check them and see if they're equivalent to the contrapositive (valid), or the inverse or converse (not valid). It's almost always a good first step to rewrite those sentences in basic "If → Then" terms when you see them. You don't have to physically write out the whole sentence; just abbreviate the key terms and use an arrow to represent the conditional relationship. For example, if (E) were in the passage, I would this in the margin: "NS → NM" (**Not Suitable → Not Miniature**).

13. Forethoughts: Typically, I go into a "weaken" question looking for an alternative explanation – something other than the thing the passage writer believes is the reason for the conclusion. Here, though, that's almost impossible for the primary part of the

---

[24] For example, people who aren't natural born citizens are ineligible, even if they meet the age requirement. So the "only if" language of the president example doesn't tell us about people who are *over* age 35; it tells us about people who are *under age 35*.

conclusion (many of our inclinations must be genetic). The psychologist has laid out some great evidence for that one. It's just hard to come up with something *other than genetics* that would explain the fact that people raised separately have so many things in common. I mean, if I see something in the answer choices that DOES explain it, that would be great, but I'm not holding my breath. But I notice there's a second part to the conclusion – not only are the traits supposed to be genetic, they're ALSO ("and") supposed to be "not subject to environmental influences." That one might be a little less unassailable; maybe they're genetic, but they're *also* subject to environmental influences. An answer choice that suggests that's true would weaken the conclusion.

(A) This strikes me as an irrelevant answer. The conclusion distinguishes between genetic and environmental forces. The problem is that while (A) notes that people change, it doesn't offer anything to tell us whether that change is caused by environment or genetics, so we don't know if the psychologist's "genetic, not environmental" explanation is supported or undermined.

(B) This is completely consistent with the psychologist's argument. The psychologist concludes that "*many*" of our inclinations are genetic; there's no reason "a few" of them wouldn't reveal differences.

(C) Irrelevant. Scientists don't need to be able to link specific genes to specific inclinations for the psychologist's argument to be valid. The argument, by citing studies that completely separate genetics from environment, is very strongly supportive of the genetic portion of the conclusion; there's no need to identify a particular "taste in clothes" (for instance) gene to validate it.

(D) Correct. Not difficult, but tricky. This answer choices doesn't attack the "genetic in origin" portion of the conclusion, but it *does* weaken the argument by undermining the "and not subject to environmental influences" portion. Growing up together and wanting to differentiate themselves is an environmental factor. If the twins put aside their inclinations toward beliefs, tastes, and career ambitions because of those factors, then their inclinations ARE "subject to environmental influences" – contrary to the psychologist's conclusion.

(E) This is beyond the scope of the passage. The psychologist's evidence pertains to identical twins, and we're told that identical twins, specifically, are "virtually the same" genetically. We're not given any information about twins who are *not* identical, so we can't assess how this answer choice affects the psychologist's conclusion. Contrast with (D), which pertains to the same group (identical twins) that the psychologist is relying on for his argument. This is another example of the inverse in a wrong answer choice. From the premise (slightly tweaked) "If two twins are identical, then they…" we can't get to the conclusion "If two twins are *not* identical, then they *don't*…"

Afterthoughts: The law, and the LSAT, is typically very, very specific. That phrase "and not subject to environmental influences" is in there for a reason, and it's part of the conclusion. Don't ignore it in your analysis.

14. Forethoughts: Combining the conditional statements in the passage should clear this one up, as long as I'm careful to translate them accurately. So, in the margin, I write: LH → LF and ~LF → ~LH (If human beings Live Happily, then Love and Friendship are their primary motives, and the contrapositive – If Love and Happiness are not people's primary motives in a society, then they cannot live happily). Next: ~LF → ENS (If Love & Friendship are not people's primary motives ("the absence of this condition"), they can have their economic needs satisfied). The common thread is when Love and Friendship are not a society's primary motives, which has two consequences – People *can't* live happily, but people's economic needs *can* be satisfied. The right answer choice will probably combine the conclusions from those two statements.

- (A) This answer choice is clearly wrong, and it's easy to dismiss if you're paying close attention. In the passage, living happily is related to whether or not love and friendship are the *primary* motives for actions, but this answer choice requires that economic utility not be a motivator at all. From the passage, there's no reason that people could be happy with economic utility as a motivator...as long as love and friendship are the *primary* motives for their actions. According to the passage, people can have other motives (besides love and friendship) and still be happy, as long as those other motives are not primary.

- (B) This combines the two threads that tie in together (happiness and economic needs, connected by the common thread of Love and Friendship as society's motives), but incorrectly. The passage tells us that it's possible to satisfy economic needs in a society where people *aren't* happy, but it doesn't tell us whether or not people can be happy where their economic needs are *not* satisfied.

- (C) Easy to dismiss at first pass – nothing in the passage talks about interactions with family members and close friends. Even to the extent that the passage talks about "love and friendship," it talks about them as primary motives within a society – not actual interactions. Also, even if you DID connect the passage to interactions with family members and close friends (in other words, we're assuming that (C) refers to the type of society in which happiness can exist, per the passage), then much like (B), above, that society may or may not satisfy economic needs – the passage doesn't tell us. This is another example of the inverse making a bad answer argument/answer choice (see questions 12 & 13, too) – the passage tells us about when economic needs *can* be satisfied; from that, we can't conclude when they *cannot* be satisfied.

(D) Correct. This connects two premises from the passage accurately – the passage's hypothetical merchant society even makes the connection directly: People's economic needs can be satisfied in that society (the passage tells us), and we know that those people would not live happily, because love and friendship are not the primary motives for their actions (in fact, they're not motives at all – economic utility is the *only* motivator).

(E) This one inaccurately combines the key ideas. Again, consider the merchant economy. According to the passage, people's economic needs can be satisfied in the merchant economy, yet they won't be happy. So the passage directly contradicts (E) and offers a specific counterexample.

Afterthoughts: Another question that really underscores the importance of untangling some of the "impure" (not written simply as IF → THEN statements) conditional statements, i.e. "only," "unless," etc. In these types of questions, most of the wrong answers invariably miscombine the key terms, and it's hard to follow the threads unless you have a firm grasp on what the passage is really saying.

15. Forethoughts: The main thing to be careful of in this sort of question (conclusion finding) is to be clear on whether they want you to recognize among the answer choices a conclusion that *could be* drawn from the passage (i.e. an inference), or identify the one that actually *appears* in the passage. The wording of the prompt is the guide. Here, "drawn in the argument" means that they've done it for you; you just have to identify it. Reading the passage, I'm looking for key words[25] to suggest where the conclusion appears; I don't want to be too lazy, though – I'm also looking for the main idea, the one that the other sentences work together to support. The first couple of sentences seem to just introduce the topic, and the last supports the third (beginning with "However"), by way of analogy. One type of infrastructure appeared rapidly, so I am supposed to infer that "this infrastructure" will, too. So it seems like the "However" sentence is my conclusion. I also want to make sure I'm clear on what "this infrastructure" refers to in that sentence. It seems pretty clear that it's referring to fuel stations for hydrogen cars.

(A) While the conclusion certainly *could* appear in the first sentence of a passage, that's not the case here. How do we know? If the first sentence were the conclusion, the remaining sentences in the passage would be used to support the initial statement. None of the following sentences is used in support of this first sentence; in fact, the first word of the *second* sentence, "But," suggests that the passage is immediately going to take off in a different direction, not continue in support of the initial sentence.

---

[25] Indicator words like "therefore," and "so" can help you find conclusions quickly, but they don't always appear in every argument, so you have to be able to do it the hard way – the logical final resting place of the argument is the conclusion; it's the point that the other sentences are working to prove.

(B) Again, this sentence (assuming "needs to be created" is a fair substitute for "does not yet exist") is not a conclusion; it's an assertion. Other statements in the passage are not used to help establish this point.

(C) This one looks pretty good (but it's wrong). This goes back to the initial question of whether we're looking for a conclusion that the passage *could* support, or a conclusion that was actually stated in the passage. We might infer that the rationale in the passage could be applied to "a new technology" in general, but the prompt asks us for the conclusion drawn *in the argument*, and that conclusion was specific to the hydrogen fuel cars ("However, *this* infrastructure...")

(D) Correct. This is the one that's right on point; we're talking, specifically, about the infrastructure for the hydrogen cars. That's what's in the passage, and, again, we can identify it as the conclusion most clearly by the fact that the sentence which follows it is used in support of it (by way of analogy).

(E) This answer choice might be close if this were an assumption question. To conclude that the infrastructure would quickly develop the way it did for gasoline-powered cars, we'd need to assume that there was a somewhat similar demand. But this isn't an assumption question; it's a conclusion question. This statement isn't drawn in the passage's argument at all. It's an implied premise, suggesting that the passage's analogy is a valid one.

Afterthoughts: If you narrowed this one down to (C) and (D), you were on the right track. Because we're looking for "the conclusion drawn in the argument," we can eliminate (C), even though it seems to fit right in with the argument.

16. Forethoughts: We have sort of a rare LSAT type of conclusion – a conclusion about what "should" be done (or, in this case, should *not* be done). In this case, the reason is essentially that helping endangered species hurts non-endangered species. So, to the extent that there's a flaw ("vulnerable to criticism" in the question stem means we're looking for a flaw), it seems like it should have to do with that comparison not being appropriate – some sort of "apples and oranges" type of thing. Maybe it's a good trade to help the endangered species out, even if it hurts the non-endangered ones. Always be wary of different things or categories that are treated as the same in an argument. Maybe it's a reasonable comparison, but maybe it's not. Also, since the conclusion is that we *shouldn't* interfere with the habitats, and since we're looking for a flaw, the right answer will give us a reason why we *should* be interfering.

(A) This is a weak answer choice on a couple of grounds. The notion that wildlife management experts "probably know best," and the suggestion that we should just defer to them is, itself, a fallacy – the "Appeal to Authority." The passage cited specific support for the conclusion. The main problem with (A) is that

"Because so-and-so said so" is a pretty lousy argument, so the idea that an argument is bad because the writer *didn't* do that…well, it's probably not going to be the "most vulnerable" thing about the argument.

(B) The problem with (B) is that it *strengthens* the argument. The passage is saying that we'd better take care of the non-endangered species – We don't want to do anything that makes it harder for them to survive. That implies that the writer IS showing concern for the non-endangered species; if they can "easily become endangered," that's not a weakness– that's all the more reason we should accept the passage's conclusion and not do anything that might harm them.

(C) This one seems either beyond the scope or irrelevant; take your pick. Come to think of it, it's also factually incorrect; the argument *does* appear to consider that saving an endangered species might be incompatible with preserving the overall diversity of species – isn't that what making it harder for the other species to survive means? Plus, (C) suggests that we shouldn't be helping the endangered species to survive; that's the writer's point! Again (like (B)), if we're going to criticize the writer of the passage, we need a reason why the experts *should* interfere (since the writer concludes that we *shouldn't*). On the other hand, the worse some of these answers seem, the more I second guess myself and wonder if (A) isn't quite as bad as I thought…

(D) Wrong comparison. The passage compares endangered species to *non-endangered* species – not to other endangered species. From the passage, it's hard to imagine the right answer won't mention non-endangered species at all; the whole basis for the argument hinges on the non-endangered species.

(E) Correct. Does the author take this for granted? Yes – the entire argument is based on the notion that if you help one type of species than you hurt another type, and for that reason, you shouldn't do it. Clearly, the implication is that it's not more important (a "higher priority") to help the endangered species, because if it *were* a higher priority, then you'd help them, even though you'd be hurting the non-endangered species. The next question is, how serious a criticism is this? Extremely. Contrast with choice (A), which might be true, but doesn't address the argument that was actually made at all. (E), attacks the entire foundation of the argument. The whole practice of identifying some species as "endangered" suggests that there might be some special reason we might want to take greater steps to protect them. The passage, though, ignores any significance that there might be to the difference between "endangered" and "non-endangered" species.

Afterthoughts: Another great illustration of a very useful practice for sorting out possibly tough questions (I'd say this one isn't a killer, but it's probably harder than most Logical Reasoning questions) – going back and seeing what the crux of the argument was. In the passage, the entire argument is about the survival of endangered species vs. the survival of non-endangered species – a conflict between the two groups. (E) is the answer choice that really focuses on that distinction. Additionally, we're looking for something to relate to a "should" conclusion; so we need something like the "higher priority" referenced in (E).

17. Forethoughts: There are two main plans of attack for a question like this; I can diagram the premises in the margin, or I can go down the list of answer choices and see if they're justified in the passage. A lot of times on these, I'll go straight to the answer choices (after reading the passage, I mean, but before doing any diagramming), but if I were to diagram out the passage, it would look something like this (using my favorite tilde ("~") for "not"): ~S&S → (CAN) DCB. S&S →~B. B→~(S&S) (contrapositive of the second sentence). Acceptable FPT = S&S OR Slow DCB growth. Some FPT → Destroy NFE (spoil/discolor quickly). The right answer choices for these types of questions will be either a combination of premises, or the contrapositive of a premise (or, possibly, the contrapositive of a conditional statement that comes from combining premises, but I generally don't expect to have to do that much work).

- (A) Incorrect. The starting point of this choice involves food preserved by an acceptable method. That means one of two things – sterilize & seal, or slow the growth of the bacteria. Obviously, slowing the *growth* of the bacteria doesn't mean eliminating it, so we might very well have food that's preserved acceptably, yet still has disease-causing bacteria.

- (B) Incorrect. We don't have enough information to know whether or not this is true. The techniques that destroy the enzymes are "some of the (food-preservation) techniques." The passage doesn't tell us *which* techniques do that – it could be the sterilizing & sealing techniques, or it could be the slowing-the-growth techniques. Or it could be some of each.

- (C) No, no, no...a thousand times, no. What do we know about the discoloring? "Some of the techniques may destroy" the enzymes that cause the food to spoil or discolor quickly. But we have no idea from the passage *which* techniques do that.

- (D) Correct, and as simple as taking the first sentence at face value: If it hasn't been sterilized and sealed, it can contain disease-causing bacteria. Period. Don't let the "acceptable method" stuff throw you. The acceptable methods involve sterilization (which we're not talking about in (D); we're talking about *nonsterilized* food) and slowing the growth of the bacteria. If all we're doing is slowing the growth of the bacteria, then clearly there can still be bacteria.

- (E) Also incorrect. Foods that are not sterilized CAN contain bacteria; that first premise doesn't state that they necessarily DO contain bacteria. So as far as we know, you can have a food that is not sterilized but also doesn't contain bacteria. It's our old incorrect friend the inverse again. If it's been sterilized (and sealed), then it doesn't have bacteria; that *doesn't* mean that if it *hasn't* been sterilized, it *does* have bacteria.

Afterthoughts: This is one where the diagramming wasn't really useful, and to be honest, I probably wouldn't have done it. I find it more efficient to evaluate each answer choice on its merits, unless there's a long passage with more interconnecting premises. But had I chosen to write out some margin notes, that's what they would have looked like. The shorthand may seem confusing at first glance, but if you zoom in on the key terms in each answer choice, and focus on the sentences in the passage that pertain to those terms, you can work through it.

By the way, when it comes to evaluating (D), don't be thrown by the "sterilized *and sealed*" in the passage, just because (D) doesn't mention sealing. The passage says it can have bacteria if it hasn't been "sterilized and sealed"; (D) qualifies, because if it hasn't been *sterilized*, then it hasn't been *sterilized and sealed*. The "sealed" part just becomes extra – if it's not sterilized, that's ALREADY enough to know that it could contain bacteria.

18. Forethoughts: I love "If and Only If" premises. You almost can't go wrong with the inferences. If X is true, then Y is true. If Y is true, then X is true. If X is false, then Y is false. If Y is false, then X is false. The only thing it looks like I have to really watch out for is the either/or thing in the last part of the premise.

- (A) This kind of looks close; if the decision is voluntary, then it's acceptable, but that's only if we're talking about activities that pose risks to live. It's not clear that he's really risking his life by not taking the car with more safety features. On the other hand, it does specify "safety" features. I don't really like this answer, because if feels like the "risks to life" bit should be more blatant. But let's say I decide I'll get back to it. You never know...sometimes you see an answer you're not really crazy about, but then you hate the next 4.

- (B) Clearly wrong. Again, assuming we're talking about risks to life, those risks would be acceptable under only two conditions – the secondhand smoke breathers would either have to bear the risks voluntarily, or get a benefit from breathing the smoke. There's nothing in the passage that says it's acceptable if the risks are "minimal."

- (C) Correct. The kind of answer that makes me feel better about not liking (A). This answer choice uses the same logic; the choice is made voluntarily (synonymous with "willingly," here); the difference is that riding a motorcycle without a helmet is much more clearly an activity that poses a risk to life than failing to replace a car with one that has more safety features (is the decision NOT to do something an "activity"? Do those safety features necessarily mean less risk to life?). This is the kind of answer that's so good, you pretty much don't have to look at the rest of the choices (in my opinion, the situations where you shouldn't bother looking at answer choices on the Logical Reasoning section are *extremely* rare).

(D) It's not clear that exposure to low levels of pollution is an activity that poses a risk to life. Moreover, non-motorists suffer from pollution, but the principle requires that *each* person who bears the risk must benefit – not just the users of motor vehicles.

(E) The passage is only about activities that pose a risk to life – when they're acceptable, and when they're unacceptable. We have no information in the passage about when activities that DON'T pose a risk to life are acceptable. Did you notice what this (incorrect) answer choice demonstrates? Yup...it's the inverse again. Activities that DO pose a risk are *unacceptable* (under certain circumstances); that doesn't mean that activities that DON'T pose a risk are *acceptable*. They HAMMER on this distinction. They give you "If P, then Q" and they check to make sure whether or not you know that "If NOT P, then NOT Q" is an invalid inference. Learn it; know it; live it.

Afterthoughts: This one isn't particularly tough. It's the kind of bread & butter question you should be able to evaluate quickly and get correct with a high degree of accuracy, mainly because 1) the passage is brief, and 2) the premises are straightforward. (B) and (D) clearly violate the simple criteria given in the passage, and (E) is beyond the scope of the passage. That leaves (A) and (C), and one is much more clearly an "activity that poses a risk to life" than the other.

19. Forethoughts: It's a "find the flaw" question, so I'm going to be reading the passage with that in mind, and hopefully be able to predict the answer. The "appearance" theory isn't really fleshed out, so apparently the flaw will revolve around the "chemical compounds" theory. The thing that really stands out to me in the passage is that in the experiment, they give "one compound" per pellet. Why specify that? Just because the predators don't mind them individually, that doesn't mean they don't deter them when they're combined; chemicals in combination do all sorts of things that they might not do individually. Could be wrong, but that's what I'm looking for.

(A) Nothing in the passage suggests that the Ecologist is presuming that the theories are incompatible with each other. The "appearance" theory is mentioned in passing; then the "compounds" theory is rejected – not because it's "incompatible" with the other theory, but because it was tested (badly).

(B) There is no reference to statistical correlation in the passage. Furthermore, this answer bears no resemblance to the predicted answer I'm still hoping for. When you're not sure about an answer choice, though, and it's one of these question types where the answers are written in general terms, look to the passage to see if the specifics in the passage match the general terms in the answer choice. Here, for instance, if I had any doubts at all about this answer choice, I'd look in the passage for something resembling a statistical correlation. There isn't one.

(C) Another answer choice that seems designed to confuse with big words. The passage simply doesn't do what (C) says. A sufficient condition is something that is enough to trigger a consequence. This is as opposed to a "necessary condition" – something that *must* occur to trigger the consequence. If a glass of lemonade costs $1, then having a dollar is a sufficient condition for buying lemonade. If you have a dollar, then you *can* buy lemonade. On the other hand, being 21 years old or older is a necessary condition or buying beer. If you *aren't* 21 or older, then you *can't* buy beer.

Here's an example of another context in which an answer like (C) would be correct. As you (hopefully!) know, you have to pass the bar exam to become a lawyer. In other words, passing the par is a *necessary* condition for becoming a lawyer. Let's say we had a (wrong) conclusion like, "John passed the bar, so he is a lawyer." That's an example of mixing up the two types of conditions. There's also a background check when you apply to become a lawyer. So John might have passed the bar, but failed the background check. Passing the bar is *necessary*, but it's not *sufficient*. That's nothing like what the passage does here.

(D) Correct. Worded a bit awkwardly, but this is the predicted answer. There is a claim that no *individual* member (a single compound) of "a set" (the chemical compounds) has a certain effect (deterring the predators), so the Ecologist has inferred (deduced) that the set as a whole (the entire group of chemical compounds the butterflies produce) does not have the effect (of deterring the predators). Or in other words – the predators don't avoid the chemicals one at a time, so they're not avoiding them in combination. Maybe, maybe not; that's a bit of a leap.

(E) The argument does not do this. The conclusion is not a restatement of the premises; it is a logical jump from the data in the premises to an assigned meaning for the data. Unfortunately, it's a *bad* jump.

Afterthoughts: This one is reminiscent of a flaw that crops up from time to time in various disguises; if you're aware of it, you're much more likely to hit on the right answer in the "prediction" stage. The flaw works in two directions, and it's essentially about the whole not being the same as the individual parts. In other words, something that is true of a group in general may not be true of individuals that are a part of the group, and vice versa. For instance, "Professional basketball players are significantly taller than most people. John is a professional basketball player. Therefore, John is significantly taller than most people." Any time there's a shift from the group to the individual, in particular, be on the lookout for something like that. If you're readily aware of that one, then things like (see passage) "...added *each* of the compounds to food pellets, *one compound per pellet*" will stick out like a sore thumb.

20. If there's one question on Test 60 that I'd say you need to understand to be a successful attorney and law student, this is it. If there's one word that best describes law – at least the study and practice of it – that word is "specific." And this is a very simple question, if you're paying attention to detail and remembering the importance of specificity. The principle pertains to criticizing others' works or actions, and it gives you two requirements for such criticism to be appropriate – it shouldn't seriously harm the person you're criticizing, and you should hope or expect someone other than yourself to benefit.

There are several specific details in that one-sentence passage – whether or not it harms someone, whether or not that harm (if it occurs) is serious, and whether or not you hope or *expect* someone else to benefit (<u>not</u>, notice, whether or not that person actually *does* benefit). What we're told in the application is that nobody benefited from the criticism. Since you should criticize only if *both* criteria in the passage are satisfied ("...AND one does so..."), in order to say that Jarrett should *not* criticize Ostertag, we need only show that one of the criteria was *not* satisfied. However, in the "Application" section, we're not told that. We're not told anything about whether Ostertag was seriously harmed by the criticism, and we're not told whether or not Jarrett *intended* to benefit someone other than himself. The right answer will be the one that clearly shows that one of the criteria justifying criticism was *not* satisfied (in which case it will be correct to say that Jarrett should not have criticized Ostertag).

- (A) Correct. Notice the difference between (A) and the actual passage. The point isn't whether anyone benefited from the criticism; it's whether Jarrett *intended* anyone to benefit. If he knew that nobody would benefit, then he could not have *intended* for anyone to benefit, and thus he did not meet the second criterion, so he "should not" have criticized Ostertag.

- (B) Look at the Principle again; remember, it has nothing to do with whether not someone will benefit – it only has to do with whether or not the person doing the criticism *hopes or expects* that someone will benefit. So this answer choice, focusing on whether or not there is an actual benefit, is irrelevant.

- (C) Nope. The criteria have nothing to do with "antagonizing" the person being criticized; there is a provision for *not seriously harming* the person, but that's a far cry from antagonizing. Plus, (C) doesn't event tell us that Ostertag was antagonized; it tells us that the criticism "might" antagonize him.

(D) This one is sneaky. One of the criteria required for criticism to be permitted is the hope or expectation that someone other than the person doing the criticizing is benefiting. That may sound as though one shouldn't criticize if the person doing the criticism hopes to benefit, but that's actually an inaccurate inference. For instance, what if Jarrett hoped to gain prestige *and also* hoped that Ostertag *would learn to write better essays*?! Then Jarrett would be hoping that someone other than himself (Ostertag) would benefit (*in addition to Jarrett*). That would actually satisfy the second criterion of the principle, and it might be acceptable for Jarrett to criticize Ostertag (providing that Ostertag were also not seriously harmed – the first criterion).

The passage says that you have to benefit somebody else; it doesn't say that you can't also benefit yourself.

(E) This answer choice doesn't show that Jarrett failed to meet the second criterion, because Jarrett might have expected that someone *other than Ostertag* (e.g. someone else in the class) might benefit. As long as Jarrett expects (or hopes) that someone other than himself will benefit, he's ok to criticize Ostertag; the person who benefits doesn't have to be Ostertag.

Afterthoughts: Don't make this one harder than it is. Carefully reading each answer choice and comparing it to the Principle should make it understandable why only (A) indicates that one of the criteria was not satisfied by Jarrett (and thus, under the conditions given in (A), Jarrett shouldn't have criticized Ostertag). Remember, the law (and the LSAT) is all in the details.

21. Forethoughts: The first thing I think about in a "Strengthen the Argument" question is the ol' alternative explanation. The writer decides that because of X, Y must be true. So I try to think of a different reason (let's call it Z) that might explain Y. What strengthens the writer's argument? If Z is *false*. Remember, the writer thinks that Y is true because of X, not Z. So anything that knocks down my alternative explanation helps the writer.

In this case, we have a simple conclusion – The reason minivans have a good safety record is that safe drivers choose them. We also have simple premises – minivans have fewer injuries per vehicle, but they don't protect you any better than other vehicles of the same size. The consultant actually did his own "alternative explanation" analysis here – from the study, he knows that minivans don't protect you better than other cars; therefore, having ruled out the "alternative explanation" that perhaps they have a good safety record because they protect you, he concludes that it must be that the drivers are safer. Not bad, but is there another possible explanation we can rule out? Even if I don't come up with a predicted answer, that's what I'll be thinking about as I evaluate the answer choices. I also try to keep in mind a very simplified form of the argument – one sentence: X is true because of Y. In this case, "Minivans have a good record for safety, because safe drivers choose them in the first place." Only one answer choice should make that sentence more likely to be true.

- (A) This doesn't help the argument, because minivans do no better in crash tests than other similarly sized vehicles. If (A) were true, safe drivers would have no particular reason to choose minivans, which would *weaken* the argument.

- (B) This one probably *weakens* the consultant's argument – if they're having as many accidents per vehicle, that doesn't give us a reason to believe that safe drivers are choosing the minivan.

- (C) This one is getting a little closer (it's the best wrong answer). If minivans don't protect their passengers better than other vehicles, and they have fewer injuries per vehicle, and they're carrying *more* people than other vehicles, then one thing seems clear – minivans are involved in fewer accidents than other vehicles. Think about it – if they were involved in as many accidents, and they weren't protecting their passengers particularly well, then they wouldn't be "the safest vehicles on the road" as measured by injuries per vehicle.

    The problem with (C) is that while it suggests that minivans are involved in fewer accidents, that doesn't tell us whether or not it's due to safe drivers choosing the minivan instead of another vehicle. If the minivan had really good brakes, for instance, that would give a reason for the fewer accidents other than good drivers choosing them, so that wouldn't help the argument.

- (D) I can eliminate this one almost without thinking about it; the passage doesn't compare or contrast vehicles of different sizes with respect to passenger protection.

- (E) Correct! The injury data and the crash test results suggest that minivans are involved in fewer accidents. The consultant claims that the reason for the safety is that safe drivers choose minivans; an *alternative explanation* could be that while they don't protect the passengers any better, maybe they have better steering or brakes, which lets drivers avoid accidents more often. That's another way (besides "safe drivers choose minivans") to explain why they have a better safety record. But if the alternative explanation is *false* (minivans steer and brake WORSE than other vehicles), then the consultant's explanation (the safety results are because of the driver, not the car) is more likely.

Afterthoughts: A good example of the "Alternative Explanation" in action. "Weaken the Argument" questions work similarly. Again, the general formula is this – the writer of the passage says, "A causes B." You try to think of C, which might also cause B (C won't be in the passage – e.g., here, the passage says nothing about the safety features of minivans). If an answer choice suggests that C might cause B, then the writer's argument is weakened; if an answer choice makes it unlikely that C would cause B, then the writer's argument is strengthened.

In this question, for instance, the passage strongly implies that minivans are involved in fewer accidents. Two possible reasons for that are 1) they have good safety features, or 2) safe drivers could choose them in the first place. *Either* of those would explain the fewer accidents. Essentially, we have two "suspects." The passage concludes that 2) is correct: Safer drivers. The reason (E) is correct is that it's the one that tells us that possible explanation 1), the good safety features, is WRONG. That's what makes it even more likely that explanation 2) – the passage's argument – is correct. Learn this thought process, know it, and live it – it's all over the LSAT.

22. Forethoughts: It's another (necessary) assumption question, and again, the easiest way to start to work through most of these is to find a term that shows up for the first time in the conclusion. If that term isn't part of the premises, then it's just about got to be in the assumption; otherwise, where would the writer be getting the information to reach a conclusion about it? Here, that term is "responsible."[26] The passage clearly shows that the government's policies have caused the gas prices to rise (Government Policies → Higher Demand → Higher Prices), but the conclusion isn't about the policies causing the increase; it's about the government's being *responsible* for the increase (remember: details & specifics!)

(A) Correct. The word "indirectly" shows up out of nowhere here...does it apply? Yes; the passage doesn't say that the government set high prices (for instance, like a minimum wage) – that would be the government "directly" causing the prices to rise. Instead, they caused an increase in demand, and that increase is what raised the prices. So it's fair to say that the advocate is arguing that the government *indirectly* caused the prices to go up. (A) connects that causation to our key word – responsibility. The negation test for Necessary Assumption questions confirms this – if the government *cannot* be responsible for things that it indirectly causes, the conclusion of the passage falls apart.

(B) This one is pretty good, as wrong answers go, but there's a key word that eliminates it – "unforeseen." Unlike "indirectly" in the previous answer choice,

---

[26] Did you catch that the first half of the first sentence (up to the comma) is the conclusion? The words "since" and "because" generally show up in sentences that include a premise and the conclusion. The premise will be on the same side of the comma as the "since" or "because," and the conclusion will be on the other side of the comma.

"unforeseen" might not apply to the passage, because we don't know whether or not the increase in gasoline prices was foreseen. Therefore, this one fails the negation test: If the government *isn't* responsible for unforeseen consequences, that doesn't *necessarily* kill the conclusion, because the increase might have been *foreseen*, not unforeseen. One thing that makes this a plausible wrong answer is that it does contain the key word we're looking for – responsible.

(C) This answer choice doesn't tie into the conclusion (the government is responsible) at all – it just affirms the link between the demand and the price. The argument doesn't require that the demand must necessarily result in a price increase; only that it did in this instance.

(D) This answer choice doesn't mention responsibility, but it does talk about the government's "obligation," which is a close enough synonym that we can't eliminate it without some consideration. Here, however, "obligation" is not being used in a relevant manner. There's nothing in the passage about the price increase being "excessive," so (D) doesn't necessarily have a bearing on this particular case. Negating this answer choice doesn't hurt the conclusion as long as the increase isn't excessive, and for all we know, it might not be.

(E) This is similar to (C), above; it's just completely off the mark with respect to "responsibility." What would have happened if the government had enacted different policies has no bearing on whether or not they're responsible for the outcomes of the policies that they *did* enact.

Afterthoughts: Remember, in *necessary* assumption questions (but not sufficient assumption questions), you confirm the answer choices by asking yourself, "What if this answer choice were false? Could the argument still work?" For the correct answer, the argument will fall apart. If you can negate an answer choice and still have a good argument, that's not the right answer.

23. Forethoughts: Just what I don't want to see in the last few minutes – a Parallel Flaw question. These are particularly complex and time consuming, because you have to not only untangle the original flaw, but also package it back up and find it in another scenario. This is one question that I'm *definitely* going to diagram; there's just too much going on to keep track of otherwise. What I might do, though, is diagram in basic letters (e.g. A→B, with "A" and "B" not standing for other things). Not only is that faster, but it actually makes it easier to pick up the same pattern in an answer choice. Here's how it would look, along with a legend as to what each letter stands for. Also, I'm going to have to pay attention to untangle some "If → Then" relationships, because I have variants here like "*Only* If."

Here's the passage: A→B. C→B. Conclusion: A→C. A = Species with frequent mutations. B = Develop Evolutionary Adaptations Each Generation. C = Survive Dramatic Environmental Changes. The key untangling is the second premise – the "only if" means that if a species *doesn't* develop the adaptions in each generation, it won't survive; contrapositively (I actually diagrammed the contrapositive), if a species survives dramatic environmental changes, then it develops the adaptions every generation.

(A) A → B. C → A. Conclusion: C → B. ("A" = Properly Built; "B" = Every stone supports another; "C" = Sturdy). Not a match.

(B) This one doesn't even qualify for symbolic analysis; I have no way of connecting the first two premises, because the second premise doesn't tell me anything about whether any plays at all are performed before different audiences every time – it just tells me that no play is performed before the *same* audience every time. A play that's not performed before the same audience EVERY time might or might not be performed before a DIFFERENT audience every time. This answer choice doesn't tell us. The passage itself may be flawed, but at least it links common terms.

(C) Correct. A = Perfectly Honest. B = Always Tells Truth. C = Morally upright. A → B. C → B. A → C. Does that one look familiar? More in "Afterthoughts."

(D) A → B. B → C. Conclusion: A → C. A = Productive. B = Well-drained. C = Good Soil. If this was your answer choice, you probably got hung up on the "only if" and/or the "unless." Remember, conditional statements can't really be dissected easily unless they're in basic If → Then form. The first premise is NOT "If it's planted in soil, then an herb garden is productive." (B → A). Don't let the "if" throw you; it's preceded by an "ONLY," so what it really means is, if the soil is NOT well-drained, then the herb garden will NOT be productive; contrapositively, if you have a productive herb garden, then you know that it's planted in well-drained soil. I'll let you similarly untangle the conclusion (with its "unless").

(E) A → B. B → C. A(?) → C. Not parallel to the original passage (and arguably not even as close as it appears; notice that "A" shifted from a healthful *diet* to a healthful *person*. But even if we make the assumption that you need to have a healthful diet to be a healthful person, the argument still wouldn't be parallel to the passage. In fact, based on that assumption, (E) is not even flawed at all.

Afterthoughts: I don't like to go too far into the "necessary" and "sufficient" language, because for the most part, I don't think it's particularly helpful. As someone once said about a chess book, "He's increased the average player's vocabulary without increasing his understanding." Here, though, it may be important to your being able to see why the passage (and answer choice (C)) are flawed. Let's look at (C) again, first. The problem is that being "morally upright" might require MORE than just telling the truth at all times. So even though you have to tell the truth to be morally upright, maybe that's not all you have to do. In other words, telling the truth is a *necessary* condition, but not a *sufficient* one.

So if you're perfectly honest, you'll never lie, but that's not good enough for us to know that you're upright. Maybe to be morally upright, you have to never lie, but you also have to give 20% of your earnings to charity. That second premise disqualifies the people who aren't honest, but that doesn't mean that everyone who IS honest automatically gets in, so the conclusion overreaches – it lets in the honest people without keeping out the ones who aren't charitable. The second premise is really the heart of the matter; it *excludes* certain people, but it doesn't automatically *include* anyone.

Our passage has the same problem. You need to develop those adaptations in each generation, but that by itself might not be good enough ("only if" keeps some species *out*, but doesn't let any of them *in*). It's like saying you'll get into Yale *only if* you get good grades. That doesn't mean that if you get good grades, you'll get into Yale; it means that if you *don't* get good grades, you *won't* get into Yale. You also need, for instance, a good SAT score. The "only" makes it a negative statement, not a positive one. Remember, "Only If" and "If" are two very different things.

24. Forethoughts: A "Principle" question asks for a general rule that governs a situation. This passage is concerned with defining the successfulness of an underground group. The critic claims that successfulness is not tied to sales. Good sales don't indicate success, because good sales might mean that the band is successful, but they might just mean that the recording is too trendy to be authentically underground. Being inauthentic, we can infer, must be a sign of *lack* of success, because otherwise, sales *would* be an indicator of success. On the other hand, *lack* of sales (possibly suggesting authenticity) still doesn't mean that the band is successful; maybe they're just incompetent. So "success" seems to be based on competence + authenticity; unsuccessfulness could mean either incompetence or lack of authenticity (or both).

(A) The critic isn't saying that a successful group *can't* sell well; he's just saying that you don't know for sure that they're successful simply because they *do* sell well. Let's say you have an underground group that's selling a ton of recordings. The critic would say that there are multiple possibilities – maybe the group really IS successful, or maybe it's a trendy recording. This answer choice doesn't fit the critic's point, because it suggests that the first possibility doesn't actually exist – a successful group won't sell very well, period. This answer choice, then, does NOT justify the critic's argument – if (A) is the guiding principle, then the critic would be wrong – sales *would* be a measure of an underground group's success, because only moderate sales would indicate success.

(B) Correct. If either incompetence or trendiness makes an underground group unsuccessful, then we can't tell anything about the group's successfulness from its sales (the critic's point) – good sales could indicate successfulness OR unsuccessfulness (in the form of trendiness); bad sales could indicate successfulness (in the form of authenticity) or unsuccessfulness (in the form of incompetence). Sales alone don't give us enough information to judge success.

(C) This is a really sneaky wrong answer choice. It's entirely consistent with the passage, because the only criterion that we know many musicians consider desirable (from the passage) is poor sales, and the conclusion is that sales are not a mark of success. So it's kind of hard to see what's wrong with (C).

The problem is, the *argument* of the passage is the link from the premises (about trendiness, competence, and authenticity) to the conclusion, about success. If we accept the principle that (C) offers us, the *argument* isn't justified (which is what the question is asking us to do) – the conclusion just restates the principle. The premises in the passage would become totally irrelevant. Contrast with (B), which links the premises in the passage to its conclusion – that's justifying the *argument*, not just handing us the conclusion on a silver platter. The argument is the jump from the premises to the conclusion – it's the connection between them. (C) supports the conclusion perfectly, but it doesn't justify the argument.

(D) This principle lays one of the conditions by which a group would be considered successful, but it doesn't purport to be an exhaustive list, and so it's not enough to get us to the passage's conclusion. (D) tells us that sometimes when a group *doesn't* sell well, it could be successful, but it doesn't tell us anything about groups that *do* sell well. So it's possible that in addition to the situation described in (D), ANY group that sells well could be considered successful. Then sales *would* be some measure of a group's success, which would be inconsistent with the passage's conclusion.

(E) The problem with this answer choice is that it makes a statement about a couple of things that are not "in themselves" marks of success. That runs contrary to the passage. The conclusion of the passage is sales are "no mark" of success, and justifies that statement with reference to other things (like competence and authenticity). If something else is required to measure success (besides competence and authenticity), maybe that "something else" is sales.

Afterthoughts: The first step is to really get at what the critic is concluding, and why. After that, when it comes to separating the answer choices that survived the first pass, it comes down the specifics. I think this is one of the tougher questions on this exam, mainly because it has a couple of pretty good looking wrong answers. A lot of LSAT questions are as easy or as hard as the second-best answer; by that I mean that even a tough passage can make for an easy question if the four wrong answers are ridiculous. What you need to ask yourself on these "principle" questions is this: If we assume that (each answer choice in turn) is true, does the passage's conclusion have to follow?

25. Forethoughts: I like these "What's the Disagreement?" questions. I know that different types of questions are easier or harder for different people, but these are pretty straightforward as long as you keep it simple. At the risk of belaboring the obvious, there are really only two questions you need to know: 1) Does each person have an opinion about this answer choice? and 2) Are those opinions different? The wrong answers will be wrong either because (at least) one of the speakers doesn't have an opinion (that we know about) regarding the answer choice, OR because they both have opinions, but don't disagree. If it sounds simple, it really is, but many students seem to frequently select answer choices that one of the speakers hasn't voiced an opinion about.

In this case, Graham offers a few points, but Adelaide specifically points out that he's "overlooked" that the computer was an extension of the programmers – people. Their disagreement certainly seems to be whether a computer (Graham's position) or human beings (Adelaide's position) deserves the credit for the computer's win. The best way to evaluate an answer choice is to ask yourself, "Would the first speaker agree with this statement?" and "Would the second person agree with this statement?" A right answer should have one "Yes" and one "No." It's really that simple.

- (A) The answer to the "Would they agree?" questions, for both Graham and Adelaide, is "I don't know." Neither of them has said anything about whether chess is "the best example" of anything. *Maybe* you could argue that Graham believes that it's the best example, since he says that if it's true for chess, it's true for "any type of human intellectual activity..." but there's certainly no indication that Adelaide believes this statement to be *false*, so we can't say that they disagree about it.

- (B) Similarly, nothing in the passage suggests either of them has an opinion as to whether chess is "typical" of the type of activities they're discussing. If we don't know what they think about it, we can't say that they disagree about it.

- (C) Correct. Graham attributes the accomplishment to the computer. The game shows that certain activities can be "mastered by machines." Adelaide attributes it to human beings; the computer was "simply an extension of the people who programmed it." We know which each party to the passage thinks about this statement, and they're not in agreement.

(D) This is the type of wrong answer that I see students sometimes go for, and I'm always a little bit surprised. It's certainly implied that Graham would agree with this statement, but there's no reason to think that Adelaide would disagree. Just because she disagrees with Graham's main point doesn't mean that she disagrees with every sub-point he's making. Adelaide's position is NOT that we can't infer intelligence from the chess computer's win; it's that the intelligence that the win reflects is that of the programmers, not the computer.

(E) Neither party addresses this assertion. Graham is specifically talking only about human *intellectual* activities that are governed by fixed principles – not "any human activity," and Adelaide doesn't address this issue at all.

Afterthoughts: Of all of the question types on the LR section of the LSAT, this is the one where it *really* pays to KEEP IT SIMPLE. What does person A think? What does person B think? If the answer to either question is "I don't know," the answer choice is wrong. If the answers to both questions are the same, the answer choice is wrong. The right answer choice will generate two definite answers, and those answers will be different.

Section 4 (Reading Comp)

PASSAGE 1

1. Forethoughts: Other than as it comes up in relation to particular questions and answers, this is not intended as a comprehensive book on strategizing for the LSAT, or attacking particular sections or question types. That being said, a general thought on Reading Comp – It is my philosophy that there is no "one size fits all" for the LSAT. Many approaches get to Rome. In my view, nowhere is that more true than in the Reading Comp section. The balance between accuracy and speed is always the key to the LSAT, and the long, dense Reading Comp passages are a challenge to find what works for you. Try different things, unless you know for sure how you're going to attack it. Try reading thoroughly, skimming, mining for the specific answer, marking the passage a lot, marking it a little, etc. For me, personally, I'm a first-time skimmer; I try to get the general themes on the first pass, with some selective marking, then I go back for the details after reading the question. That's in line with my general philosophy, which is that I don't want to burn too much time making sure I could answer questions that might not even be asked. General forethoughts for this first passage and question are pretty straight forward – Suburbia has negative effects on communities, per the New Urbansists. So...on to the answer choices.

- (A) Even if this were true, it's not going to be the answer. First of all, it's very specific in nature; it's not a "Main Point" sort of answer – it would be one detail of many. Second, it's against the theme of the passage, which (although also providing an opposing point of view) primarily *explains* the New Urbanist position – it's not a critique of New Urbanism; it's an introduction to it. So the main point won't be critical. I'd eliminate this answer almost without bothering looking to see if the statement is even true (if I didn't remember). It's not, by the way – the passage lets us know that New Urbanists *do* consider the interests and values of those who prefer the suburban lifestyle – lines 50-55.

- (B) On general principles, this is a candidate. The part about inhibiting the social interaction is certainly true; but my quick read through the passage wasn't enough for me to really remember whether they advocate specific zoning laws. I didn't think so, but I do remember something about zoning. This one would be put on standby for a second pass. If the other answer choices are as bad as (A), I'm not going back to the passage. As it turns out, we'll have another good answer choice, which later sends me back to the passage, where I don't find anything about advocating specific zoning reform, so this choice will be eliminated at that point.

(C) I don't remember this being true, and it's probably too specific to be a main point. I might take a quick glance back at the first two paragraphs, just because I remember the word "gratifying" coming up. At this point, I would go to the passage, because I already have another candidate answer, so I have to do some differentiation. I skim and find "gratifying" in line 39, but it's not in the context of answer choice (C) (nor do I find any other specific reference to "most people" finding it "generally more gratifying"), so I eliminate (C).

(D) Correct. This is the other serious candidate answer. It's general ("a corrosive effect on community life"), and it's consistent with the passage in that it's an introduction to what New Urbanism is all about. The only question about (B) vs. (D) (at this point, I still haven't eliminated (B)) is which specific point is accurate – the zoning reforms referenced in (B), or the developing recommendations referenced in (D). (D) sounds better as I recall the passage, but I'm going to take a look and try to find the details for sure. Sure enough, there it is right in the section I just looked at to eliminate (C) – a section I noted in the margin as "they advocate" (lines 36-43). The general theme of (D) is on point, and the details are confirmed in the passage. I almost always look at all answer choices in the Reading Comp section, but I might actually move on here without looking at (E).

(E) Having just refreshed my reading of the passage, I know that it's a different type of development that the New Urbanists advocate, not a different traffic policy. The traffic is referenced heavily in the passage, but it's a *symptom* of the development – because the homes and businesses are only connected by collector roads (lines 26-30). They don't suggest changing the traffic policies; they suggest changing the layout that *causes* the traffic.

Afterthoughts: "Main Point" questions are kind of bread-and-butter questions. If you at least skim the passage, you should have an idea what it's about. The main point should be general, possibly with some supporting specificity (such as, in this case, the "development modeled on small urban neighborhoods"). The right answer will also be consistent with the tone of the passage, unlike (A), in this instance.

2. Forethoughts: Some of these, especially with the time factor, are essentially a test of how well you remember the passage (assuming you read it first). If you remember the right answer, or think you do, then it's a lot faster to find something specific than it is to reread the passage coming up with the answer for the first time. The detrimental result I recall from the passage is that when people are all in their own cars, they don't interact with each other. Hopefully, there will be an answer that looks like that, so I don't have to track down a bunch of different possibilities.

(A) I don't remember anything about the financial burden, and even though it's not a "Main Point" question, this doesn't feel right. The passage is all about people socializing, and how that's a function of the neighborhood. I'll skip it for now, and come back to it if I think I have to. Seems like a really unlikely candidate.

(B) Again, this isn't ringing any bells. The passage isn't about "productive employment." To the extent that employment is mentioned, it's about how the workplaces are all together, separated from the homes, and that's why people are in cars. But the result of the cars is that people aren't walking around, hanging out, talking to each other, etc. This is a first-round pass, also.

(C) This sounds good. I don't specifically remember "antisocial behavior," but by definition, being isolated in a car is not "social," so it sounds good. For the first time, I'm going to go to the passage and see if I can justify this answer choice. Yep! Lines 29-35. Verified by quickly scanning the passage looking for key words to match the answer choice. Particularly, "driving" and "antisocial."

(D) Having found obvious support for (C), above, I would not seriously consider (D), and might not even look at it. If you read lines 29-35, there should be no doubt that (C) is correct. Having said that, air pollution is not singled out in the passage. But it's not worth the time confirming that (D) is wrong after evaluating (C). You just don't have time to even skim the passage 5 times for each question.

(E) Similar to (D). The time that would be spent outside the car is specified in the passage as "involv[ing] social interaction within a physical public realm," not time spent with one's children. It might be *true* (just as the air pollution thing might be true), but it's not in the passage.

Afterthoughts: You've just got to save time when you can on the LSAT, especially in the reading comprehension section. The best way to do that, when possible, is to recognize when an answer has a good chance of being correct, THEN going back to the passage to confirm. (A) and (B) didn't sound plausible to me, so I was able to save time by not referring back to the passage until I hit (C), and since (C) was correct, I again saved time by not having to check up on (D) or (E). Alternatively, you might have looked specifically for the travel section of the passage, found the answer, and then looked for it in the answer choices. Either way works. What you don't want to do is read (A), look for it in the passage; then read (B), look for it in the passage; etc.

3. Forethoughts: No really great way around these "strongly suggests they would agree with" questions. You pretty much have to know the passage, or at least get a standout answer choice that is obviously correct. Also, without looking at the answer choices, there's no way to "preview" what the correct answer will be. So, just hit the answers, choice by choice, and hopefully we'll be able to recognize one, or at least eliminate a few.

(A) This doesn't sound right. You don't have to remember everything from the passage (for almost all of us, that would be impossible), but you do have to have a grasp of the main theme. Here, for the New Urbanists, it seems to be about quality, not quantity. The problem isn't the amount of time they spend getting from one place to another; it's that they spend that time in a car, not interacting with one another. My general approach on these, in deference to the sliding scale between time and accuracy, is to pass over the ones that feel wrong (without rereading the passage over and over to verify or eliminate), and hope to come across answers later that seem right, then just double-check a more limited sample of answers. This one seems safe to eliminate out of hand.

(B) This is better than (A), for sure. The New Urbanists clearly feel that we're uncivil as a(n indirect) result of zoning laws. It's not so clear that they'd agree that we can't do anything about it. This answer isn't obviously right (in fact, as it turns out, it's not right at all), but it's not as "obviously wrong" as (A), so I'm going to move on to (C) with the understanding that (B) is now the answer to beat. Now that I've found a better answer than (A), (A) is off my horizon altogether.

(C) Definitely not. If people living in suburban neighborhoods didn't have trouble finding jobs that didn't involve commuting, we wouldn't have a problem to discuss; the whole passage is predicated on the idea that people in suburban neighborhoods *do* have to commute.

(D) Correct. At first reading, it was not obviously apparent (to me) that this answer choice is correct; your mileage may vary. But it sounded right, so it sent me back to the passage, but now with a specific mission – to confirm one particular answer choice. The obvious half of this answer choice is that it influences the attitudes of the people who live in them. That's the main thrust of the passage – the influences that the layouts have as a result of the commuting, isolation, etc. What I want to look for is the other direction in the answer choice – the notion that the layouts *are influenced by* people's attitudes. That's found throughout the third paragraph – people's "legitimate desire to secure the enjoyment...etc." The New Urbanists specifically comment that neighborhood layouts do reflect people's values (lines 53-55). I'm now comfortable in rejecting (B), and I'll take just a quick look at (E), expecting to be able to dismiss it.

(E) Fairly easily dismissed after rereading (ok, reskimming) that third paragraph. The New Urbanists aren't saying don't build in accordance with your values; they're saying, "Think about your values, and recognize that there are hidden costs to the consumer lifestyle." They seem to want us (as a group) to change our values, and build according to 'better' values.

Afterthoughts: Very often, due to time constraints and answers that seem to be more about "shades of gray," the Reading Comp section becomes a running reevaluation between answer choices. Is (A) better than (B)? Is (C) better than whichever was better between (A) and (B)? How does the new "best" answer compare with (D)? And so on. To the extent that you're able to make most of those choices in your head without revisiting the passage, you'll help cut down on the time pressure that can really strike hard in this section. Ideally, you'd love to find the right answer without going back to the passage at all, but it seems like most of the time, that doesn't happen. But if you can limit your time going back to the passage to where you're either confirming a single "best choice," or differentiating between the two best choices, you'll be on your way to effectively maximizing your time investment. Sometimes easier said than done.

4. Forethoughts: Now, this is the kind of Reading Comp question I like. Direct me to a specific portion of the passage every time! Ok, let's go back and compare the two uses of the word "community(ies)." The first one is a group of buildings/zones/uses, etc., and the second – the "concept of community" – is the more personal definition, with people interacting, etc. ("communing," as it were). Should be fairly straightforward.

- (A) Clearly incorrect. The words have entirely different meanings at the indicated lines. Don't let them tell you the LSAT "doesn't measure knowledge." Some questions (this one, for instance) are straight-up vocabulary tests.

- (B) Correct. Stone-dead-exactly 100% on the money. On a real LSAT, if you're comfortable with the vocabulary, you could circle (B) and go to the next question.

- (C) There's nothing in the passage to indicate that it means that the communities of Line 2 are to be "defined in terms of the interests of their members." Also, the "concept of community" reference in Line 15 doesn't refer to people who have "something else in common." Why would that require a town square or local pub? Those types of places are needed to give people a chance to interact with one another – regardless of whether they have things in common.

- (D) The Line 2 definition is clearly off again. The "low-density communities" are geographic areas of buildings and people; they don't have to have "professional or political ties." The Line 15 definition is markedly worse; read line 15 in its entirety – why would it be "hard to imagine" community without a town square or local pub, if all 'community' means is people who live near each other?

- (E) Both uses are misdescribed yet again. It's not groups of people who specifically have "informal personal ties" that have proliferated at the edges of cities; it's actual little neighborhoods. And again, at line 15, you don't need a town square or pub to group together "people of similar backgrounds and lifestyles."

Afterthoughts: If you know the nuances of the word "community," this is an easy question. If you don't, then you're going to have to struggle through the context. The Line 2 context is broad – what's springing up at the edges of the cities? Little-to-midsize residential towns – dwellings and people in those dwellings. They don't have to have common interests, informal ties, or professional/political ties. They just all have to want to (and be able to afford to) live close enough to the cities themselves to drive into work, but far enough to avoid pollution, crime, or whatever else they're trying to avoid. Then there's Line 15; what definition of "community" makes it hard to imagine without a town square or local pub? The one that is based on their just being out and associating with each other…talking, interacting…hanging out – a "sense of belonging together."

5. Forethoughts: Almost like a Logical Reasoning question – which would weaken the position? The best we can do, probably, is just make sure we have a firm grip on what the position of the critics is. Seems pretty straightforward – see lines 46-50. Those lines make it clear that the position of the critics pertains specifically to one thing – why the people who live in the suburbs choose to do so (for reasons given in that section of the passage). The logical reasoning technique of looking for an alternative explanation may serve us well here; what else might explain it?

- (A) Seems to be off-point. The critics don't offer a position on the differences between people in the suburbs and people in the cities; they offer an explanation for why some people live in the suburbs. The expression of their legitimate desires, etc. etc.

- (B) Again, how would this weaken their position? The critics didn't say that most people who drive long distances to shop live in suburbs. This answer choice does not address, much less undermine, the point attributed to the critics.

- (C) The other side of the answer choice (B) coin…and still off-point. The critics of New Urbanism (at least in the passage) aren't offering opinions on who has to drive the farthest for entertainment and shopping.

- (D) Correct. Notice that for the first time, we have an answer choice that directly undermines the critics' assertion – they don't live in the suburbs because they love that whole car culture thing; they live there because it's what they can afford.

- (E) The most irrelevant of 4 irrelevant answers. The critics aren't commenting on who votes in municipal elections and why.

Afterthoughts: I wasn't crazy about this question at first, for an instructional point, but the more I looked at it, the more I liked it. It's a good reminder not to over-think questions. This question asks about a very specific point – the critics' position. The passage frames the critics' position very specifically – it's about why people live in the suburbs. Only one of the five answer choices pertains to that. Keep it simple, and if you get stuck, be guided by the question, or the part of the passage the question points you to. Even if you don't understand the critics' position, it should be clear that it's not about comparing the suburbs and other areas; it's about *why* people live in the suburbs. Only one answer choice is on that point. It's no coincidence that it's the right answer.

6. Forethoughts: In a reading comp passage, I'm pretty safely expecting not to have to guess or infer too much. If the question is "most strongly suggests," then the right answer should be pretty explicit (how fast and reliably it can be found...that might be another question). Just like the last question, I want to go straight to the source. So, let's see the recommendations of Duany and his colleagues: Lines 36-45 (My margin note, "They advocate" directs me to the right spot). Two possibilities suggest themselves – the change in actual character of the neighborhoods (i.e. what would be built: the cafes, stores, schools, etc. in walking distance); and the interaction and mutual respect.

- (A) A few problems with this one. First, "eliminated" is an awfully strong word. Most importantly, though, this kind of answer choice is asking for more speculation than I expect to have to do. Again, I'm looking for one of two things – the type of neighborhood, or the mutual respect. That's what was in the passage in the section that talked about what the New Urbanists wanted to see. Not speculation about what would happen with zoning laws.

- (B) This one would be another stretch. I could talk myself into believing that it's true, if I engaged in a great degree of extrapolation, but could this answer possibly be the one "most strongly supported" by the passage? Nothing in lines 36-45 talks about the percentage of buildings that contain a particular number of residents. A "most strongly supported" answer choice should fit much more directly with what's *actually stated* in the relevant portion of the passage.

- (C) The passage suggests that this answer is false. The current scheme is that living and shopping areas are built in separate areas (lines 11-12). If the mix of businesses and residences that the New Urbanists advocate were built, then people would spend *less* time traveling for shopping and work, not more – places to work and shop would exist in their own neighborhoods.

- (D) Again, "eliminating" makes me skeptical, and again, asking for an inference about zoning policies...that's too much of a stretch for "most strongly supported." The passage "strongly supports" two types of conclusions – what the neighborhoods would look like, and the personal interaction between people who live in those types of neighborhoods.

- (E) Correct. The suburban communities are going to have both grocery stores and neighborhood schools (lines 41-42). They don't exist now, because zoning laws require people to travel to "separate areas" (lines 10-12), so the "gratifying mix" that includes schools and grocery stores will represent an increase.

Afterthoughts: Just like question 5 – the correct answer is the one that comes directly from the passage. Keep it simple, and especially if the question is difficult, be guided by the details of the passage. When you find "schools" and "grocery stores" in the exact portion of the passage that the question directs you to, that's a sign. When the other answer choices don't have the same sort of match, that's even better.

7. Forethoughts: That second paragraph is just too big to give me much of a predicted answer. I always try to predict an answer when practical, and questions that direct me to specific ideas (like question 6), or specific lines, are good candidates. But a question like this, which references a 27-line paragraph, well...that's a different story. So I'm not going to waste time starting at the paragraph – I'm going straight to the answer choices.

- (A) Correct. Looking at the paragraph with this answer choice in mind, I have to do a double–take at the first part of the paragraph. It's easy to miss the relevant portion. The statement that there's a "de facto economic segregation" because of similarly priced homes is the tip-off. This portion of the passage suggests that neighbors will be in the same economic stratum because the houses are the same price. So, for instance, if you make enough money to qualify to buy a $500,000 house, and you buy one, you're going to live with people of your same economic means. But that assumes that most people, like you, are going to buy the most expensive house than can afford. You might have a neighbor who makes 10 times as much as you, but maybe he'd rather save more for his retirement, or go to Hawaii 2 months every year, rather than put all of his money into a $5 million house. That's answer choice (A) – if someone is paying "drastically less than he can afford," then he (that's the neighbor in my example, not you) is NOT "economically segregated" just because the houses are the same price.

- (B) This is essentially the exact opposite of the New Urbanist position. When the passage says that there's a "de facto economic segregation," it's specifically saying that the suburbs are NOT "economically diverse." In other words, rich and poor people never live in proximity to each other, which is bad for society (children are ill prepared for life in a diverse society – see lines 23-26).

- (C) While we might surmise that this is true (or we might not; it's certainly not clear), it's not an assumption that underlies the New Urbanists' argument in the way that (A) does. The New Urbanists suggest that motorists are anti-social towards each other, and pedestrians are not, so we should have zoning that encourages more pedestrian activity. There's not really a pedestrian-vs.-motorist discussion; instead, we have a comparison between polar opposite schemes – one in which we're all motorists, and another in which we're all pedestrians.

(D) Pretty much directly contradicted by the passage. See line 29 – residents are "forced" to drive to carry out their daily tasks; clearly, per the passage, they're not doing so because they're unaware of health benefits.

(E) This is consistent with the second paragraph, but it's not an inference that's really strongly supported by it. The passage says that the suburbs contain houses that are almost identical in price and appearance, but it doesn't say *why* that is. Maybe it's for the efficiency and convenience of the developers, who can crank out new developments faster and cheaper by making all the houses essentially identical.

Afterthoughts: It can be a real time-saver to have an idea of whether or not predicting an answer will be worthwhile (You don't really want to spend 30 or 40 seconds thinking about a predicted answer only to realize that you can't come up with one). As a general rule, consider how broad the question (or its source material) is. If the question could come from anywhere in a huge paragraph, forget it – get straight to the answer choices; if it's more specific, it's probably worth spending a little time thinking about what the answer might look like. Other than that, notice that two of the four wrong answers are specifically contradicted by the passage. Be attuned to answer choice like these; they should be easy to quickly eliminate. The passage doesn't require an assumption that's inconsistent with its claims.

PASSAGE 2

8. Forethoughts: The passages are both descriptive – they describe a history, rather than trying to persuade the reader. The common ground obviously includes bees, as well as some specific discoveries, as well as naming the scientists who made them.

- (A) No…these guys are scientists; what does it even mean to have "human-like" intelligence? The descriptors in these passages are far too specific. Their communication might be symbolic, hearing-based, etc. But "human-like" is too vague. Neither of them uses a characterization like that. *I* might think that some of the things that are described sound "human-like," but it would be a stretch to claim that the writers of the passage are trying to argue that point. Moreover, they're not really "arguing" anything; they're describing.

- (B) Definitely not, as long as you've had enough biology to know that bees are not primates. We're looking for an aim that the two passages have in common; the only animals that Passage A looks at specifically are the honeybees, so anything about primates is not going to be common ground.

- (C) Correct. This one looks good from the start. They both describe scientific studies, and the studies deal with animal communication. Unlike answer choice (B), which is limited to primates, this choice talks about "animals," which is broad enough to include honeybees.

    In two separate (non-LSAT) recent discussions, I've heard something like, "They're not animals; they're insects." Biology freebie to go with the LSAT stuff: Insects _are_ animals. What the heck are they teaching kids today, anyway?!

- (D) While some of the experiments revealed that previously held beliefs were in error (like the Gould discovery first mentioned in lines 26-29), there's really nothing that would be construed as a "scientific controversy." It seems, instead, like the typical advances of science, with new discoveries disproving old hypotheses. I have some sympathy for this answer choice, but it's really not as good as (C), partly because (C) is much more direct, and partly because "controversy" implies something much more than "disagreement."

- (E) The only mention of language is in the von Frisch paragraph (lines 49-55), wherein the author of Passage B notes that von Frisch called the bees' communication a language. The passages, however, don't get into the purely semantic discussion of what constitutes a language. It's about how animals communicate; not whether that communication should be called a "language."

Afterthoughts: Fairly straightforward. This is similar to one of those Logical Reasoning questions where you're asked to find the point at issue between two speakers. The real key is just to be sure you're clear as to what each speaker is saying independently; you can't treat the passage as one big whole. If it's missing from one of the speaker's portions, then it's not going to be the right answer. As long as you remember that you're reading two separate, small passages, and not one large one, it should be manageable.

9. Forethoughts: Having just reviewed the passages, it's fresh in my mind that Passage A was all about bees, and Passage B discussed various animals (answer choice (B) in question 8, about the primates, reminded me of that). There may be other differences, too, in the nature of the experiments or the interpretations. The "types of animals" thing is the obvious one that comes to mind, but I may have to look for other specific differences, depending on the answer choices.

- (A) First answer out of the box, and it's pretty much dead on. I know that Passage A only talks about honeybees, and I know that Passage B talks about other animals (such as the vervet monkeys). On a timed exam (like a diagnostic or the actual LSAT), this would be another of those rare Reading Comprehension questions where I'd be comfortable not even looking at other answer choices. Great opportunity to have a high percentage answer (this must be over 90% without even looking at (B) through (E)) and save time, too.

- (B) Passage A does discuss some of the evidence; the problem with this answer choice is that Passage B also discusses some of the evidence, as well. For instance, the last paragraph cites Gould's experiment. The first paragraph also talks specifically about what was observed with respect to vervet monkeys – this is the evidence that supports the claim that they communicate symbolically (line 39). So both passages discuss the evidence, and choice (B) is therefore incorrect.

- (C) I find this answer choice to be a little ambiguous; it has a couple of possible interpretations, but both can be dismissed. When it says that Passage B is "entirely about recent theories of honeybee communication," on its face, that's clearly incorrect, because some of Passage B isn't about honeybees at all (for example, the first paragraph, about the vervet monkeys). More likely, this answer choice should be taken to mean that to the extent that Passage B is about honeybees, it's only about the recent theories. However, this interpretation is incorrect, also, because the second paragraph discusses historical hypotheses (like Wenner's – lines 53-55) that have since proven to be incorrect. Notice that Passage B doesn't tell us when Wenner's hypothesis was developed (maybe it was "recent," even though it's been disproven), but Passage A suggests that Wenner's research (he was uncovering things in the 60's – line 13) was probably old enough not to be considered "recent."

- (D) For time saving purposes, by the way, it's a good idea to try to disprove these answer choices by referring to Passage B, since it's the shorter passage. As long as what an answer choice says about Passage B is incorrect, the answer choice is going to be wrong, regardless of what it says about Passage A. Here, for instance, Passage B isn't "concerned" with explaining the distinction between symbolic and nonsymbolic communication. Other than mentioning very briefly that some animals may communicate nonsymbolically (e.g. ants leave trails, line 36), the passage is entirely concerned with describing symbolic language. Since I know that (D) is wrong about Passage B, I don't need to hunt through the longer Passage A to see if (D) is right about Passage A.

- (E) This is almost a "bluff" answer choice. There's no reason at all to think that this is correct, because there's nothing at all in Passage B to suggest that it's concerned with human communication in *any* respect. Don't fall for stuff like this. The right answer choice will be reflected in the passage. You may have to do a very small amount of translating, looking for synonyms, etc., but the material in the right answer choice will be found in the passage. Nothing from (E) is found in Passage B, so you can dismiss this answer choice with confidence.

Afterthoughts: This was one of the easier reading comprehension questions. If your instincts or your reading led you to (A), this is a good illustration of how you should trust your instincts. If they didn't, then you either need to reread the passage (if it was an understanding issue) or ask yourself how you got talked out of a fairly straightforward correct answer (if it was an LSAT issue). It's certainly easy to misread something in a hurry, or to second guess yourself; however, because the content in this question/answer pair was so direct, this question is a good point to stop and consider to make sure you're at least thinking about the passage correctly.

10. Forethoughts: You should love the questions that direct you to specific places in the passage. They save time, and they improve accuracy by telling you exactly what to focus on. The great thing about this question is that Passage A tells us almost nothing about Gould – it's very narrow. He got bees to send other bees to places that the first bees hadn't been, thereby showing that odor is not necessary to their communication. Conversely, Passage B tells us that bees *couldn't* get other bees to go to places that they actually HAD been, when there were no pollinating flowers there. There's not much else that can be in the right answer; what we know about Gould is too limited.

- (A) This answer choice is inconsistent with Passage A, which tells us that the fact that foragers send bees to places the foragers haven't been demonstrates that they *don't* need to use olfactory information (odor). This is one of the things that's annoying about the LSAT – they'll tell you that it doesn't test knowledge, but if you don't know what "olfactory" means, you're in trouble here (it means related to the sense of smell). Without the olfactory information, Passage A says they still followed the foragers' signals, which is contrary to answer choice (A).

(B) This is inconsistent with Passage B, which tells us that forager honeybees directed other honeybees to a location (the boat on the middle of the lake) where there were no pollinating flowers. Those instructions were ignored, but the claim that they won't dispatch their nestmates to any other place is false. This is a subtle yet important distinction, and hopefully it didn't trick you. If you chose (B) because Passage B says that the other bees wouldn't *go* to the boat where there were no flowers, you're close to the right track, but (B) isn't about whether the bees would go there; it's about whether the foragers would try to *send* them there. This shows one of the (few) ways in which the LSAT is good preparation for law school – little distinctions can matter a lot.

(C) You don't have to make stuff up on the LSAT, especially when the question directs you to very specific parts of the passage. We have very few lines that are dedicated to Gould. Nothing in them says anything about whether the forager bees in question are "experienced" or not. This answer choice can't be right. "Only," by the way, is one of the most important words on the LSAT. Pay close attention when you see it.

(D) Correct, and dead on point. The first part of the sentence (drawing other bees to sites the forager hasn't visited) is straight out of lines 26-27, and the second part is from lines 58-62. Take another look at those portions of the passage, and make sure you fully appreciate how directly the language in the passage corresponds to the answer choice. This is common in questions that direct you to specific portions of the passage – there's just generally not all that much of a reach that you need to make; it's right there. On an actual LSAT, this is definitely obvious enough that I wouldn't bother to read (E).

(E) This is not shown in Passage A. The portion that deals with Gould doesn't talk about the trail. It is suggestive of Wenner's hypothesis (lines 23-25 – the trail would presumably be the odors conveyed from the food source), but the passage goes on to say that Gould showed that they don't need odor to communicate. Also, Passage B doesn't mention odor with respect to Gould's findings.

Afterthoughts: Generally, the easiest questions to answer in the Reading Comprehension section are the ones that limit themselves to specific portions of the passage. Here, everything we need is going to be found in the two small portions of the passages (one in 'A' and the other in 'B') that talk about Gould. As long as you look carefully at those two portions, and don't add anything, this should be a very straightforward question, and, better yet, one that isn't too time consuming. There's just not that much rereading you might even have to worry about.

11. Forethoughts: In contrast to the last question, here, we're going to have to possibly do some thinking/reaching beyond the passage – the question is asking to *infer* (i.e.

read between the lines) from the passage. Moreover, the right answer choice will pertain to things found in *both* passages; we can't just take a statement that's true for one of the passage and assume that's our right answer. There's too much going on in both passages to predict a correct answer here, since the question isn't limited to specific lines or contentions. We'll just have to evaluate each answer choice on its own merits.

(A) Passage A (as we analyzed previously, for example in evaluating 10 (A)), goes against this answer choice. Gould showed that forager honeybees don't need odors to send other honeybees off to food sources. We can disprove any of the answer choices by finding it to be inconsistent with either passage; for it to be correct, it needs support from *both* passages; if it lacks support from *either* passage, that's good enough to cross it off our list and move on.

(B) Passage B doesn't mention Esch at all, and only briefly mentions Wenner. To the extent that it *does* mention Wenner, it's inconsistent with this answer choice. The author of Passage B believes that Wenner was WRONG when he claimed that smell ("olfactory clues") plays a part in the bees' communication (lines 53-55). So the author of Passage B would NOT accept that Wenner "established" it; Passage B says that answer choice (B) is an *incorrect* belief that Wenner had.

(C) There is no basis for concluding that the author of Passage A would have any particular opinion about animals other than bees. Passage A is only about studies on bees and their communication. The conclusions are a result of specific experiments done with bees. It would go too far beyond the scope of Passage A to take those findings and apply them to other species.

(D) Correct. Both passages mention Von Frisch, and both passages are consistent with this answer choice. In lines 49-52, we see clear support for this position in Passage B. In Passage A, the support appears in lines 7-11. Von Frisch didn't answer all of the questions, but his work certainly was fundamental to the growing body of knowledge – he and his colleagues not only figured out that the bees' dance was a form of communication – they cracked the code and figured out where the food was!

(E) This answer choice calls for total speculation. The passages are concerned with how the foragers communicate with the non-foragers, but there's nothing about how the foragers learn the language that they use to communicate. It may sound perfectly reasonable, but there's no evidentiary basis (in the passage) that suggests that it's true. Remember, the question says "It can be inferred *from the passage...*" We can't just make it up, no matter how obvious it sounds.

Afterthoughts: Nothing too tricky here. The key is to make sure to find support in *both* passages. An answer choice that is dead on point with respect to one of the passages but not mentioned at all in the other is going to be incorrect. Check answer (C), for instance; you might reasonably conclude that the author of Passage B would accept this statement, but there's no support for it at all in Passage A, so it can't be right, no matter how good it sounds in light of Passage B.

12. Forethoughts: This is going to be another one that will require looking at the answer choices to evaluate them (as opposed to predicting an answer), but clearly, the basic difference between the passage is that Passage A is all about the honeybees, and Passage B is broader, discussing honeybees as one of various animals that the passage applies to.

- (A) These sorts of answer types (putting specific passages into general terms) crop up a lot in the Logical Reasoning section, as well. Essentially, you just try to locate the specific portions of the passage that might correspond to the general answer choices. For (A) to be correct, for instance, we need to find a "position" in Passage B that Passage A rejects. It's just not there. The passage discusses specific experiments, but the only real "position" it takes is that all animals communicate in some sense. Passage A doesn't claim that some animals don't communicate (that would be the only potential "rejection" of the position taken in Passage B), so this answer choice doesn't fit.

- (B) Again, to find the general terms of the answer choice in the passage, what "phenomenon" could this answer choice be referring to? Animal communication? No, Passage B offers multiple examples. There's no phenomenon that meets this description (exemplified several times in Passage A, but only once in Passage B), so this answer choice doesn't fit, either.

- (C) Correct. Is there a phecnomenon that Passage A is concerned with in its (Passage A's) entirety? Yes – the communication methods of honeybees. Does Passage B discuss honeybee communication? Yes. Does Passage B do so "in support of a more general thesis"? Yes – Passage B's thesis is its first sentence: All animals communicate. In the course of supporting that thesis, Passage B discusses the one thing that Passage A is concerned with in its entirety – the communication of honeybees.

- (D) There is no phenomenon that Passage B argues cannot be plausibly explained, so this answer choice is incorrect. There is some speculation involved in some of the experiments (e.g. we don't know for sure why the bees ignore the foragers' directions to the food in the boat), but Passage B does not say that it can't be plausibly explained; on the contrary, Passage B offers an explanation – the other bees know that there are no pollinating flowers growing there (lines 63-64).

- (E) The primary concern of Passage B is animal communication. Passage A does not provide a historical account of the origins of animal communication. The reference to Aristotle doesn't suffice here, because Aristotle was only making an observation about bees (not the primary concern of Passage B), and, moreover, the Aristotle reference doesn't tell us about even when bees started communicating – just the first time (apparently) that someone noticed.

Afterthoughts: You have to try to find what each word or phrase in the answer choice might refer to, in order to see if the answer choice fits. What phenomenon? What's the primary concern of Passage B? What position is put forth in the passage? What's the more general thesis? To the extent that you can identify these potential components of the passage, you'll be able to find the one that fits…and the four that don't.

PASSAGE 3

13. Forethoughts: In general, I first look to the end of the first paragraph for a "main point" question (assuming I haven't already developed what I think is the main point in my head). Here, though, it seems that the main point is the last sentence of the whole passage, because the other paragraphs don't support the first paragraph; they continue it and modify it. So I'm basically looking for something that credits Valdez, but not exclusively – the passage's last sentence makes clear that it was a group effort.

(A) This is a potentially tempting wrong answer choice. First, there is a subtlety with respect to the term "some." With respect to *reading comprehension*,[27] I take that term to connote "more than one." That's the everyday meaning. If you had one child, you wouldn't say you had "some children." The passage cites only one historian (Broyles-Gonzalez, lines 40-41) as challenging the view in question. Moreover, the view discussed in paragraph 3 isn't identical to the view expressed in choice (A) (sole credit for inventing actos vs. not being "influenced" by earlier forms), and in paragraph 3, historians "tended to credit" Valdez; in (A), the view is claimed to be "widely accepted," which is a significantly stronger claim.

Most importantly, even if the views of paragraph 3 and answer choice (A) are construed as identical for the sake of argument, and even if "some" in answer choice (A) could mean "one," there's still a big problem with (A) – it's not the *main point* of the passage. Answer choice (A) says that historians are challenging a previously held view, but the passage isn't an objective discussion about the state of theatrical critiques – the main point of the passage isn't that challenges to convention wisdom are arising; it's that those challenges are *correct in doing so*. This is a <u>persuasive</u> article – the point isn't that it's newsworthy that Broyles-Gonzalez is criticizing historians; it's that she's *rightly* criticizing them (line 41). The author clearly has a position here, and that position will be expressed in the main point; the main point isn't about what "some historians" are saying. The bigger takeaway point we can learn from this question is, it's important to pay attention not just to the factual content, but also the tone of the passage.

(B) Chavez is mentioned as the topic is introduced, and there is clearly a parallel time frame between the Chicano labor movement and the theater development, but there is nothing in the passage about Chavez's deserving more credit in the development of the Chicano theater movement. The author clearly believes that

---

[27] In the *Logical Reasoning* section, "some" means "at least one." That's the formal logical meaning. I haven't come across any LSAT prep materials that address this point, and as far as I know, I'm just making up the distinction on my own, but I cannot recall a Reading Comp question on the LSAT that was based on a reference to "some" being singular (in contrast, there are many Logical Reasoning LSAT answer choices that are right or wrong because of a single example qualifying as "some").

Valdez should not get full credit for the Chicano theater movement, but the missing credit shouldn't go to Chavez, but rather to the actors' contributions, and also to the earlier forms of theater – the carpas (lines 43-54). The author relies heavily on Broyles-Gonzalez's claims, and her claims (at least as presented in paragraph 3) do not suggest that it is Chavez who should be getting more credit.

(C) Correct. This is essentially what I had in mind. The broader "main point" of the passage really comes together in the third paragraph. The first two paragraphs are more historical, tracing the relevant developments. The paragraph outlining Broyles-Gonzalez's book illustrates the author's main point, because, as pointed out in the analysis of (A), above, the author is endorsing Broyles-Gonzalez's point of view. The passage explicitly states that the early development was a "collective accomplishment," (54-56) the first part of Answer Choice (C), and also that Valdez's contribution was "crucial" (56-57), pretty much as close as you can get to saying "essential" (the second part of Answer Choice (C)) without using identical wording. This answer choice is pretty much spot-on target with the mid-last part of the third paragraph, which is where the main point of the passage is.

(D) This is true, but it's not the main point. The author believes that Valdez does not deserve *sole* credit for the success and creation of Teatro Campesino, but his contributions are still a major part of it. If the main point was all about the amateur performers, the passage wouldn't finish by emphasizing Valdez's importance (lines 56-60). If Valdez really isn't a part of the main point at all (he's not a part of Answer Choice (D) at all), then would the very last sentence of the whole passage include a clause like "Valdez's artistic contribution was a crucial one"? No; the passage would have closed with the Broyles-Gonzalez criticism of the historians, not gone back to re-emphasize Valdez's contributions.

(E) The passage doesn't at all emphasize Valdez's "political and academic connections," nor does it go into the "recognition" that the Teatro Campesino received. The first paragraph mentions Valdez's connection to Cesar Chavez, but that connection isn't linked (in the passage) to the Teatro's recognition; the only "recognition" mentioned in the first paragraph is the recognition of the UFW – Chavez's group. And that recognition came from the boycott of grapes, not from any political-theatrical affiliation.

Afterthoughts: What readers remember, generally, is the first thing they read, or the last. For this reason, main points are generally found in the beginning of a passage (first paragraph, though often at the end), or at the end of a passage. Think of papers you may have written; you probably led with your main point, then supported it, or you laid out your evidence, then wrapped it all up at the end with your main point. Both are good approaches, and (not coincidentally) common ones. Generally, you can eliminate the choices that are either not true (or not supported), narrowing down the choices to a couple of possibilities. Here, for instance, (C) and (D) might make the final cut; then you can focus on where the emphasis in the passage is.

14. Forethoughts: This is a good news/bad news question. The good news is, it's a question that has a specific line reference. That's a time saver, and it helps accuracy, too. We don't have to look around different parts of the passage trying to figure out what's going on. We know exactly what we need to focus on. The bad news is, this question illustrates one of the big lies about the LSAT – that it doesn't test knowledge. Especially in the Reading Comprehension section, the LSAT is, from time to time, a vocabulary test. If you know the connotation of "immediacy" here, you're probably in good shape, and if you don't, this could be a tough question. Knowing what "palpable" means would help, too. Finally, the last clue is going to be the first half of the sentence – "Because *actos* were based on participants' personal experiences." "Palpable" means either tangible or readily apparent, obvious, clear...something along those lines.

"Immediacy" could mean a few things. The obvious one that you might guess or already be aware of is related to "immediate." Something that has to be done right away. But it doesn't make sense that something like that would have to do with the actors' personal experiences. It might also pertain to physical closeness, but that doesn't make sense, for the same reason. The "closeness" that's being implied by this use of "immediacy" is a closeness of awareness or understanding. Here, "immediacy" means something that's clearly and directly understood. This isn't any convoluted "artsy" kind of symbolic theater – it's real-life stuff (based on their personal experiences), and because of that, the audience "gets it." The audience has no trouble at all relating to the show. That's what we're looking for.

- (A) Incorrect. If you know that there is a definition of "immediacy" that pertains to physical closeness (you might think of something that's "immediately to the left of couch," for instance), then you might be tempted by this answer choice, but you have to consider context. The actors' personal experiences won't have anything to do with the physical distances between the actos and the audiences, so this answer choice doesn't fit.

- (B) "Sense of intimacy" is close to the definition I'm looking for, but this stuff about addressing their lines to the audience is coming out of nowhere. It doesn't say in the passage that they did that. Plus, even if they did, the sentence in question tells me that the cause of the immediacy, again, is that the material is *based on their life experiences*, not whether or not they talk to the audience directly. Better than (A), but not a great answer choice.

- (C) We seem to be kind of touching on what we're looking for, but not really hitting it dead on. The context of the sentence does tell us that the Teatro Campesino members' own experiences are relevant here, but it shouldn't have anything to do with how easily they were able to include their experiences into their work. Take an actor like Anthony Hopkins, who reportedly was a serious alcoholic. If he plays a character where he can tap into those experiences, it might have a real impact on the audience – an *immediacy*. But it's not because it's "easy" (if it is) for him to incorporate those experiences into his acting; it's because he's HAD those experiences and can convey those emotions. There's a reality to it. And if he can share the depression/loneliness/despair that he knows with his audience, it's going to have a big impact, whether it's easy for him or not.

(D) The fact that the performers have actually had these experiences would not have an impact on how closely they work with the director to build a repertoire of actos. Like the other wrong answers, above, this answer choice can't really be connected to the context of the sentence. It presents an idea that just doesn't relate to the first part of that key sentence – the real-life nature of the actors' experiences.

(E) Correct. The immediacy refers to the actos' being vividly conveyed to the audience. Something "vivid" is palpable – it's realistic. And why were they able to vividly convey these experiences to the audiences? Because they had actually *lived* them. They were "based on the participants' personal experiences." It's the difference between someone reading you a newspaper account of a tragic story, and hearing the story firsthand from the survivor. That direct experience they had with the material is the basis for the connection with the audience. How vividly did they convey that experience? So vividly that it created a *palpable immediacy* – The audience immediately and clearly understood what it was like.

Afterthoughts: As it turned out, this question wasn't really as much of a vocabulary test as it might have been. Everything really came down to the context ("...based on participants' personal experiences..."). So the afterthought here, really, is don't despair if you don't know the meaning of a word; check out the sentence in its entirety, and, if need be, the whole paragraph. There are more clues than just the word itself.

15. Forethoughts: Another question that pinpoints a specific part of the passage. If you have trouble on timing in the Reading Comp section – say you're running out of time on the last (or even the third) passage – these are the best questions to aim for, becausy You'll be able to evaluate them faster. The second sentence gives some historical context to the passage, by explaining the political backdrop at the time. This is going to connect to the theatrical stuff, because the first paragraph will go on to connect the two, through Valdez's association with Chavez, and the significant "anchor" year 1965, which figured into both the labor movement, and the birth of Teatro Campesino.

(A) Correct. Your mileage may vary, but for me, this isn't one of those bells-and-whistles-go-off-instantly answer choices that tell me at first glance that I've got the right answer, but at least it sounds plausible. Read the third sentence – Teatro Campesino was about *using theater to organize farm workers*. Don't get caught up in the story about how the art developed; the art was a vehicle for political purposes. So the motivation to get support for the unionization of farm workers is a relevant driving factor, and it's also an important aspect of their subject matter, because as we've seen above, the workers' lives WAS the subject matter of the Actos. I'd consider this a good answer choice at first glance, but I'd go on to the others and see if there's another I like better.

(B) Definitely not. What major obstacle? Getting the growers to sign union contracts? That was Cesar Chavez's problem, not Valdez's. And there's nothing in the passage that suggests that it had anything to do with public acceptance of Teatro Campesino. There's no suggestion that the line pertains to any sort of "major obstacle" that Valdez had to deal with.

(C) When you see general catch phrases like "counters a possible objection," you should try to match it up to specifics. What possible objection might this counter? The position referred to in this answer choice is that Teatro Campesino was effective political theater, so if line 2 counters an objection to that position, then somehow, line 2 would have to support the *effectiveness* of Teatro Campesino as political theater. But all line 2 does is talk about what Cesar Chavez was doing at the time. We haven't even gotten to Valdez and Teatro Campesino yet, so how can this counter an objection to its effectiveness as political theater?

(D) Again, there's just no justification for this in the passage. One of the key points of the Reading Comp section in particular is not to reach outside the four corners of what they give you. Nowhere in the passage does it tell us that scholars of Mexican American history have typically focused on other things to the exclusion of theater history. It's not even suggested. In fact, the final paragraph includes a critique of what "theater historians" tend to do, so we know that theater history isn't being ignored – there are actual historians who specialize in it.

(E) Contrast this answer choice to (D), above. Here, the answer choice correctly refers to theater historians, and also correctly identifies something that they tend to do – give Valdez sole credit for developing the actos. The reason this is a bad answer choice, though, is that if we limit our analysis to the second sentence of the passage (as the question asks), nothing in that sentence that explains why the theater historians do what they do. The second sentence is about Chavez organizing farm workers; how does that possibly explain Valdez getting all the credit? No connection at all.

Afterthoughts: Two key techniques both come into play on question 15. First, don't import any outside information into the question. It's fairly easy to eliminate an answer choice like (D) if you remember that the correct answer must come from the passage alone. The passage doesn't state or suggest that theater history was ignored. Second, remember to focus on the key parts of the passage that the question directs you to, where applicable. Here, we're directed very specifically to the second sentence of the passage. So even an answer choice like (E), which accurately describes some of what's happening in the passage, is incorrect – because the second sentence, which is the only sentence we're evaluating, does not explain what the historians are doing.

16. Forethoughts: My recollection is that there is more in the passage about actos than there is about carpas, so I'm going to focus my attention on the carpas. Since there's not that much about them, it should just take a few seconds to get a complete rundown of what the carpas were all about (since I certainly don't remember from my initial reading of the passage). Once I know what the passage says about the carpas, I'll see which of those things is also true of the actos. Looking back, I see that all the passage tells me about the carpas is they were: informal; often satirical; performed in tents to mainly working-class audiences; and came out of Mexico and the United States (or at least flourished there) (lines 47-51). The actos are described in the second half of the second paragraph. Skimming over that part of the second paragraph looking for the key terms that apply to the carpas, I see that the actos, too, were satirical (line 36). I got the impression that actos are informal, also, but the one thing that passage clearly states is true of both actos and carpas is their satirical nature, so that's what I'm going to be looking for first. If I don't find it, I'll see if anything else sounds right.

- (A) Nothing in the passage tells me that carpas had their roots in European theater – in fact, lines 58-59 suggest the opposite, by contrasting carpas to traditional European theater. By saying that actos were *neither* carpas *nor* traditional European theater, the passage is telling us that carpas and traditional European theater are two different things.

- (B) The carpas are only mentioned in the third paragraph, and there's nothing there about the San Francisco mimes (that group was mentioned in the second paragraph, as part of Valdez's background). So this is not a match. The passage doesn't tell us or suggest that the mimes were related to the carpas in any way.

- (C) The carpas were performed "in tents" to mainly working-class audiences, but the passage does not tell us that they were initially (or ever) performed on farms. Don't import that idea into the passage; if it's not there, it's probably not the right answer. There are places other than farms where you could set up a tent to show theater to working-class audiences.

- (D) Correct. This is the one I was looking for. The support for this answer is directly in the passage – no reaching required (lines 36 & 47). Having reviewed the criteria of the carpas and then checked them against the actos, I might have skimmed the answer choices looking for this from the beginning, which would have saved some time had I been confident enough to just circle it and move on. That wouldn't be a bad approach on this question, because the information about the carpas is so limited, and the only thing that clearly matches the actos is the part about satire. For the purposes of this book, though, I'm looking at each answer choice as if it were being considered.

- (E) Nothing in the discussion of the carpas suggests that they were part of union organizing drives. They were shown to "working-class audiences," but it's a big jump to go from that to assuming that they were part of union organizing drives.

Afterthoughts: Again, to the maximum extent possible, in the Reading Comp section, you don't want to go outside the passage; you want to take your answers directly from the passage itself. Here, there's one answer that has explicit support in the passage, and four that don't. Even if some of those wrong answers seem to be consistent with your reading of the passage ("working-class" sounds like it goes with "union organizing," for instance), you don't want to make those leaps unless you absolutely have to. When might you have to? If the passage explicitly asks you speculate (sometimes you get questions like, "Which of the following would the author of the passage *most likely* agree with?"), or if you can't find direct support for any of the five answer choices in the passage. Your first line of attack, though, is to find the answer that is clearly expressed in the passage. Here, that's answer choice (D).

17. Forethoughts: This is one that will probably require us to go outside the passage – we have to *infer* something. As such, there's no real way to predict what the correct answer choice will look like. Valdez, no doubt, had all sorts of views; we'll just have to look at these five possibilities and see what fits.

- (A) This answer choice doesn't fit, for a couple of reasons. First, we know that Valdez endorsed the actos and their use of satire (see previous question), which the carpas shared. Second, the last sentence of the passage confirms that the actos did have elements of the carpas; why would they, if Valdez thought they were ill-suited to what he was trying to create? Third, the performers adapted the carpas to their performances (lines 53-54). The actos weren't carpas, but there was certainly overlap, so calling them "ill-suited" doesn't seem to fit.

(B) This is a better fit than (A), in that we know that Valdez *did* want to use the theater to organize farm workers; that's why he approached Chavez in the first place (lines 11-12). But we don't have any reason to believe that Valdez thought that Chavez didn't do enough in this regard. I guess if the other four answers were all horrible (like answer choice (A)), I might think about (B) with the rationale that, "Well, he probably wanted all the help he could get," but it sounds pretty unlikely. This isn't really a good answer choice; it's just better than (A).

(C) There are (at least) two possible ways to interpret the passage in light of this question; both of the two that come to my mind suggest that this is not a good answer choice. First, we could dismiss this answer choice out of hand, because the passage doesn't specifically refer to avant-garde theater, so we can't say with any confidence what Valdez would think about it. Alternatively, we do know that Valdez had traditional European theatrical training (lines 58-59); we could speculate that that included avant-garde theater. Even making that leap, though, we don't have any reason to accept this answer choice, because nothing in the passage suggests that Valdez rejected *any* influence as "irrelevant." In fact, the passage tells us that the actos had connections to Valdez's European training. So, either the passage doesn't suggest *anything* about avant-garde theater, in which case (C) is wrong, or it suggests that Valdez may have had training in European avant-garde theater – and the actos had a variety of influences, including the roots of Valdez's training...so (C) is, again, wrong.

(D) Correct. We can reasonably infer that Valdez, a student of theater and an actor himself, would not spend years of his life doing something he didn't think could be effective or artistically successful. Yet when he went to form Teatro Campesino, he did not recruit trained actors; he recruited farm workers. So he would presumably agree that formally trained actors are not required for effective, successful performances.

(E) He might very well agree with this, as an artist and a student of art. The fact that he wanted to use his art for political purposes doesn't *necessarily* mean that he thought that art had to be evaluated in terms of politics. But the question is asking us what can be inferred *from the passage*. The passage doesn't tell us either way how he thinks theater's aesthetic aspects should be evaluated. We'd have to guess. Contrast this with (D); the passage doesn't explicitly state that (D) is true, but we can go by the fact that Valdez recruited people who were not formally trained actors to draw a likely inference. To evaluate (E), though, we'd be making a pure guess.

Afterthoughts: Even in this question, which asks us to speculate, the correct answer is the one that doesn't require us to reach far beyond the four corners of the passage.

There is concrete evidence in the passage that tells us that Valdez specifically did something that suggests that (D) is correct. The more you resist the urge to stray from the passage in the Reading Comp section, the happier you'll be.

18. Forethoughts: This should be pretty straightforward, for a couple of reasons. First, the question specifically tells us that our answer is supposed to be **based on the passage**. That's how we like 'em. Second, it's asking us for the area of agreement between the author and Broyles-Gonzalez, and Broyles-Gonzalez is only mentioned in a very narrow portion of the passage (beginning of the third paragraph). So we have an extremely limited portion of the passage to worry about, which is always a good thing for both speed *and* accuracy. The clue is the word 'rightly' in line 41. That's a clear sign of the author's agreement with Broyles-Gonzalez. What he's agreeing with is that Valdez shouldn't get sole credit for developing the actos, because the Teatro Campesino actors were also influenced by the carpas.

- (A) Careful...this one might catch you, especially if you're working quickly. The agreement between the author and Broyles-Gonzalez *does* pertain to the carpas, but it isn't about the influences that shaped the *carpas*; it's about the way the carpas shaped the *actos*.

- (B) Classic illustration of how you can confidently eliminate a wrong answer by limiting yourself to the scope of the passage. Yes, the portion of the passage that cites Broyles-Gonzalez is about historians and their exaggerated claims about the amount of credit that should be due Valdez, but the passage does not suggest that Broyles-Gonzalez has a particular motive in mind. She *is* making a claim about what the historians have wrongly done, but she *isn't* claiming to know the reason why they've done it.

- (C) Correct. Both the author and Broyles-Gonzalez agree that the carpas were very significant with respect to the development of the actos. Broyles-Gonzalez *traces* the connection of the actos to the carpas; the carpas came first, and the participants of the actos "had cultural links" to the carpas, and "likely adapted" them to their performances in the actos. That makes the carpas quite significant for the development of the actos. We know the author agrees with Broyles-Gonzalez, because the whole part about the carpas is a more specific look at why Broyles-Gonzalez criticitzes the historians – because they give Valdez sole credit, improperly, for the development of the actos. Instead, Broyles-Gonzalez believes, they should recognize the other influences that the Teatro Campesino participants had, *especially* (lines 46, then 46-54) the carpas. And according to the author, this credit that Broyles-Gonzalez seeks to spread around is done "rightly" (again, line 41).

(D) The passage doesn't comment on whether or not Broyles-Gonzalez believed Valdez was familiar with carpas, or to what extent. This is easily verified, because she's only mentioned in the last paragraph. The author relates some of Broyles-Gonzalez's views on Valdez, and some of her views on the carpas, but nothing on how familiar Valdez was with the carpas. Broyles-Gonzalez's point was that the carpas influenced the *actors performing the actos*, not Valdez (lines 51-54).

(E) This might be a tempting answer choice; the author believes, and points out in the relevant paragraph, that the traditional European training influenced Valdez, but a careful reading shows that by the time the European training is mentioned, the author has stopped talking about Broyles-Gonzalez's position, so we don't know whether Broyles-Gonzalez would agree. The last paragraph flows like this (from the author's point of view) – 1) Broyles-Gonzalez says, correctly, Valdez shouldn't get sole credit. 2) Broyles-Gonzalez supports this position by pointing to the carpas. 3) The author emphasizes, in conclusion, that while Valdez shouldn't get sole credit, he still played a big role – his European influences were also apparent in the actos.

Afterthoughts: The more narrowly you can limit the portion of the passage you focus on, the faster and more accurate your analysis will be, (assuming that limitation is justified!) Here, we know that we need Broyles-Gonzalez's position on something; there's no "agreement" without her. Since the author's positions are strewn throughout the entire passage, and Broyles-Gonzalez's positions are in a very limited portion of the passage, the best way to evaluate this question is by focusing on the portion that discusses her position.

19. Forethoughts: The wide-open nature of this question tells me that this question can only be answered by a choice-by-choice analysis. At least by now (having answered four questions about this passage already), I'm getting a better feel for the passage and its salient points.

(A) I don't remember anything about farm owners "accepting" efforts to organize. Just that bit about Chavez's trying to get the growers to sign union contracts. This answer doesn't sound right, based on my initial reading and subsequent re-visits to the passage to answer questions 15-18, so I'm not going to spend time trying to prove a negative, i.e. rereading the whole passage to assure myself that there's not a sentence in here that would support this choice. I'm just going to move on to the other choices and expect to find something that fits better. Part of doing well on the LSAT is getting questions right; another part of doing well is being able to save 20-30 seconds here and there, so you start feeling the time crunch at question 23 instead of question 17 (or wherever).

(B) Again, I don't have any recollection of anyone other than Valdez being referenced as a former mime (and, frankly, my general mindset as regards farm workers is that they're a really hardworking, busy bunch of people who probably don't have a lot of free time to study mimehood. No offense intended to any mimes (or farm workers) who may be reading). Part of time management in the Reading Comp section involves being able to initially pare down answer choices from memory or "gut reaction," to minimize the number of times you have to actually reread parts of the passage. If you did go back to the passage on (B) (or (A)), you probably found that the passage doesn't support either answer choice.

(C) Correct. This is the first answer choice that sets off that little bell ringing in my head. Not because I remember this question being answered directly, but because the timing sounds right to support it. It's that 1965 thing...the United Farm Workers, as I recall, were already in full swing as the Teatro Campesino was just getting started, which means Teatro Campesino probably couldn't have played a major role in the United Farm Workers' "earliest" efforts. That's from the first paragraph, so I'm going to go back to the passage now, for the first time, as confirmation. Yes...there it is – In 1965, the United Farm Workers had "gained international recognition." Meanwhile, Valdez is approaching Chavez, and the Teatro Campesino will "result" (line 13) from this effort; so, clearly, Teatro Campesino could not have played any kind of major role in "earliest" efforts of the United Farm Workers; Teatro Campesino came later.

(D) On an actual LSAT, I would decide that (C) has so much support that I would not look at (D) or (E) (another way to save 30 or 40 seconds). For the purposes of evaluation, though, let's take a look at (D). I don't remember anything in the passage about whether performances were in English or Spanish, or them changing at any point in time. Skimming the passage will confirm this, but I think that would stand out enough that I'd remember it, so I wouldn't bother going back to the passage to verify that this one is wrong.

(E) I don't think this is right, either, but unlike the other wrong answers, this one does trip a small wire in my memory, about the United States and Mexico. I'd go back to the passage to find what I was remembering, and confirm that it doesn't support this answer choice. What came to mind was from lines 49-51, about the carpas flourishing in the border areas between Mexico and the United States. That satisfies me that what I was remembering wasn't anything that would suggest that (E) was correct, so now I can commit to (C) with a clear conscience.

Afterthoughts: These "wide-open" question types can really eat up your time if you you second guess yourself too much. They're entirely unlimited in scope, so reading over the whole passage five times (once for every answer) can be burdensome. The way to manage that threat to your timing is twofold – First, have the confidence to dismiss some answer choices without rereading the whole passage to make 100% sure that there's not a single word in there that might support the answer choice. Second, try to be familiar enough with the passage so that if you *do* have to refer back to it to check out an answer choice, you have some idea of where you're going to look. For instance, here, I know that if an answer choice is about Broyles-Gonzalez, it's in the last paragraph. If it's about Cesar Chavez, it's in the first paragraph. And so on. Part of that comes from just paying attention as you read, but it can also be very helpful to make notes off to the side of the passage identifying the key subject matter of each of the paragraphs.

20. Forethoughts: Another one of those "most strongly supports" questions with nothing to narrow down the subject matter or limit it to a specific part of the passage. You know the drill by now...get to the answer choices and evaluate them one by one.

- (A) Since I just reread that U.S./Mexico reference in evaluating answer choice (E) to question 19, above, I know that it refers to where the carpas were flourishing. But that doesn't tell me that theater historians have widely discussed or analyzed the tradition of carpas. In fact, I have a reason to suspect that's *not* the case – if the carpas tradition had been widely discussed and analyzed, then it probably wouldn't be true that the historians would be giving Valdez sole credit for the actos; the historians would be aware, as the passage's author and Broyles-Gonzalez are, that the actos were heavily influenced by the carpas. Apparently, that connection has escaped the historians (which is why Valdez gets all the credit for the actos), so I'm led to believe that if anything, the historians have mostly *missed* the significance of the tradition of the carpas.

- (B) Correct. I don't remember much about comedy in the passage, but it is a part of satire, and there might have been some mention of it in the middle paragraph. This answer choice is worth another look at the passage. Checking the bottom of the second paragraph (lines 31-39), the acto was the quintessential form of Chicano theater in the 1960s (there's my connection to the 1960s, part of (B)), and the actos include "a brief comic statement" and satire. So it does sound like comedy was a prominent feature of Chicano theater in the 1960s – it was integral to the single genre (actos) that is attached to that decade. Good answer choice.

- (C) This doesn't sound right, because my recollection (which is borne out in the passage in lines 17-22) is that the participants were just acting out what they'd experienced. So why would Valdez have had to go to "great lengths"? More importantly, with respect to the carpas, we're not told *what* audiences had experienced in them. So how would we know what "certain aspects" were simulated or recreated? This is fairly easy (and not time-consuming) to check, because the reference to carpas sends me directly to the last part of the last paragraph – which I know is the only place in which the carpas are discussed.

(D) This is directly contrary to the same portion of the passage (beginning of the second paragraph) referenced in (C), above. There's no mention of Valdez writing scripts. He "asked them to talk" about what it was like where they worked. He asked them to "illustrate" what happened in the picket lines. The content sprang from the actors themselves; Valdez (apparently) just adapted those presentations to a theatrical format (skits) that he was familiar with.

(E) This just comes out of nowhere. I read the passage initially, and I've reread (ok, reskimmed) parts of it quite a few times as I've assessed the answer choices of previous questions, and I don't remember anything remotely like this. I might skim the passage looking for "1970s," and if I do, I'll find that the Chicano theater movement reached its apex in the 1970s, but there's nothing there (lines 14-16) or anywhere else about Valdez moving on to other endeavors.

Afterthoughts: There's nothing too tricky or unique about this question. In addition to hopefully getting it right, the best you can do is not spend too much time checking out all the different answer choices. Again, this means having the confidence to eliminate some choices immediately, and really being able to limit your search on other ones. For instance, with respect to (A) and (C), I know that carpas are only discussed in the last paragraph. With respect to (D), I know that the "earliest actos" are going to be discussed at the beginning of the second paragraph, because I know how the passage is laid out. You just can't afford to keep going over the whole passage every time.

PASSAGE 4

21. Forethoughts: If I've paid attention or marked the passage, then I'll expect that this answer will be found at the beginning of the second paragraph; that's where the recommended uplift agreements are mentioned. The gist of what's recommended is so straightforward, I may not have to refer back to the passage – the uplift agreements that are recommended are the ones where, if the case is a winner, the lawyer gets his usual rate plus an agreed-upon *rate increase*. So, instead of a typical American contingency fee, where an attorney might get, say, 1/3 of *all* money recovered, in one of these "uplift" agreements, if the lawyer wins the case, and his usual rate is $300/hour, he might get $360/hour (usual rate +20%), regardless of how much is actually recovered. Now, I just have to find an answer choice that sounds something like that.

- (A) This isn't parallel to the fee structure in the passage. That passage describes a single fee rate that will be increased by a fixed percentage. Here, we have various rates being paid out for different people who "joined together" and contributed. The passage doesn't describe multiple contributions. Also, this lottery example contemplates paying out the entire amount of the award (lottery). In a contingent fee arrangement, the plaintiff gets some of the money, and the law firm gets some of it.

- (B) Correct. Unlike (A), we have a single entity (the consulting firm) getting paid – just like in a contingency case, one law firm will be paid. Also, the firm only gets paid if successful – another key element of a contingency fee arrangement. Finally, the fee isn't increased by the amount of the client's profit (which is how we think of contingency fees in the USA: bigger award = bigger payoff to the lawyers); instead, the fee is increased by a fixed amount ("will be paid double" = usual fees are being increased by 100%). This fixed increases matches the passage (lines 15-17 – an "agreed-upon additional percentage" of the fee).

- (C) This has the same basic problem as (A) – we're not dividing the returns among many different entities (partners, in this case) at different rates of payment. The passage is describing a single, pre-negotiated payment rate that is going out to a single entity (the law firm representing a plaintiff).

- (D) This is one of those answer choices that seems designed purely to distract you. Sometimes people fall into the trap of assuming that if an answer choice doesn't make sense, it's correct. The passage recommends fee agreements that are clearly and specifically outlined. In contrast, this answer gives a pretty vague description of how costs are determined. If you try to determine how it might match up to a contingent fee agreement, you should notice that it's not really parallel at all. For instance, what would the cost of the insurance policy match up to? Presumably, it could only potentially be the cost of legal fees. In the insurance industry (and as outlined in (D)), that cost is determined by the "likelihood and magnitude of an eventual loss." So, for instance, the amount I'm willing to pay for auto insurance is determined by 1) how likely it is that I'll need it; and 2) how much *it will cost me* if I do. But contingent fees are just the opposite – I think about how much I stand to *gain* if I win my case. And if I do lose, I don't have any legal fees at all – this, too, does not match up to the insurance model, where I still have to pay my premiums regardless of whether or not I have an accident.

(E) Buying insurance, again, is a poor analogy in any case. As noted in (D), the buyer has to pay premiums whether or not the default ever happens. Moreover, the price of the premiums doesn't have any specified basis in (E) at all; the passage is all about laying out in great detail the way the cost of the legal fees is determined. Contingent fee legal agreements are about finding a creative way that a client can *benefit* from pursuing a claim that he would not be able to afford to otherwise pursue (due to the high cost of legal fees). They're for people who can't write the big check up front, but could really use a lawyer. Risk avoidance (the essence of insurance) is not comparable. In fact, it's kind of the opposite – you pay up front, because you're afraid of having to write a big check later.

Afterthoughts: Another pretty good illustration of how useful the strategy of limiting your examination of the passage is. The subject of question is "the uplift fee agreements that the LRCWA's report recommends." That wording leads us straight to the beginning of paragraph two (lines 12-14), and if we read just the rest of the sentence that mentions that phrase, we find exactly what the right answer should look like – 1) successful outcome; 2) lawyer's normal fee; 3) additional agreed-on percentage of the fee. (B) has all of those things; none of the other answers really comes close. And it comes from just one sentence in the passage, which the question directly leads us to. Keep it simple.

22. Forethoughts: This is a wide-open question; the passage states a lot of things. So there's not much we can do in the way of pre-work; we just have to hit the answer choices one at a time, and hope that we can get to the right one quickly and confidently.

(A) Correct. This one is a gimme if you get to the right part of the passage. In the last paragraph, the passage discusses why the reasons for contingency fees apply to all clients, and then sets forth exactly what those reasons are. Number two (lines 52-55) is that they transfer the risk from the client to the lawyer. In other words, pursuing a lawsuit is expensive. Without a contingency fee, the client has to spend a lot of money, and the risk is that he won't get a verdict, so all that money will be lost. With a contingency fee, though, the lawyer spends money (mostly in the form of time) pursuing the case, and if there's no recovery, the lawyer doesn't get compensated. So the risk is shifted to the lawyer. This one is such a direct hit that you could certainly move on to question 23 without worrying about (B) through (E).

(B) If you're not sure about (A), then you're going to have to consider the other answer choices. The best you can do, probably, is to limit your search. If you remember something about fairness, you may be drawn to the first part of the second paragraph (because of this choice's word "deserve"), which mentions that the uplift fee agreements are "*intended to* prevent lawyers from gaining disproportionately..." While that sounds like a plausible near-match to (B), there are at least two problems with it -

A potential small problem is that it's not clear that "gaining disproportionately" (the passage) is a perfect match to "larger fees than they deserve" (answer choice). If I spend 10 hours on a case (ridiculously small figure designed just to keep the math simple), and you're hoping to get $10,000, but I get you a million dollars, and our agreement is that I get a third of it, then I've certainly "gained disproportionately" (even good lawyers don't make $33,000 an hour), but is it necessarily "unfair"? Even after paying me, you've made $650,000 more than you'd hoped for. Man, I'm good!

The other problem with (B) is, even if we accept that "gaining disproportionately" is "unfair," the passage doesn't state that the uplift fees don't necessarily prevent that unfairness; it says that they're INTENDED TO prevent it.

(C) This answer choice receives no support from the passage. There's no specific place to refer to, because the passage doesn't directly contradict this claim; it simply doesn't include it, except for one thing in the passage that mildly argues *against* (C) – the repeated use of the word "would" rather than "will" (lines 32, 43, 44, and 45) – the consequences to the proposal are all written hypothetically, because the passage is not claiming they will be adopted. The only real question about this answer choice should be how long it takes you to eliminate it.

(D) The passage states that this answer choice is incorrect – allowing contingency fees *would* affect lawyers' diligence. In particular, contingency fee agreements make lawyers more committed and more diligent (lines 57-60). The problem with the proposal isn't that it changes the nature of contingency fee agreements; it's that it limits their availability. Contingency fee agreements (per the passage), including "uplift" fee agreements, DO affect lawyers' diligence and commitment (for the better). So the passage specifically states the exact opposite of (D).

(E) This question is testing to see whether you fall into the trap of importing any outside knowledge to the test. You may believe that contingency fees are a set percentage of the plaintiff's award (a pretty good assumption, in the USA). You get hurt in a car accident, you hire a lawyer to sue the person who hit you, and the lawyer gets a quarter, or a third, or whatever percentage of your damages. That's how we think of contingency fee agreements in the USA. The only problem is that it's not in the passage. The passage merely says, very generally, "there are various types of contingency-fee arrangements," and then it goes into detail about one of those types, the uplift fee arrangement. The passage offers no details or comments about how the "usual" contingency fee agreement is structured. If this was your answer choice, I sympathize, but the question was, "**The passage states** which one of the following."

Afterthoughts: A question that begins "The passage states" shouldn't be that hard, but there are a few traps for the unwary. There's a possible loss of time chasing an answer choice that's nowhere in the passage at all (C); the danger of importing your own knowledge of the subject matter (E); and the possibility of misreading an answer choice that contains subject matter that's in the passage, but reaches the wrong conclusion (D). Counterintuitively, the best defense may be to stop reading once you've found the answer choice that actually does appear in the passage. It's clear that the statement in (A) is found in the passage, so why spend extra time and risk second-guessing yourself out of the right answer by looking at (B) through (E)?

23. Forethoughts: This one shouldn't be too challenging, because the passage is fairly straightforward. When possible, I prefer having a predicted answer in mind, to avoid distracting answer choices, so I'm going to take just a few seconds to try to formulate one in my mind. Essentially, the passage seems to be to inform as us to what the recommendation of the LRCWA is, and to persuade us why it isn't good (because it doesn't go far enough – it only permits a small segment of potential plaintiffs to benefit from contingency fee agreements).

- (A) This one doesn't fit. The passage is about *introducing*, rather than *reforming* contingency fees – currently they aren't allowed at all (in Western Australia). Playing devil's advocate for a second, it *could* be considered a reform to the legal system as a whole – the change from not permitting contingency fee agreements to permitting one type. The real problem with (A) is that it isn't *defending* the proposal at all. The passage itself is a strongly-worded *criticism* of the proposal.

- (B) Also incorrect. The passage is about the LRCWA proposal, not the current legal system. Remember, the proposal being discussed is just that – a proposal. The passage is about the merits of the recommended change, which is not currently in place. It's true that the author's preference – opening the legal system to an even wider array of contingency fee agreements – *would* represent a change to the legal system, but the passage is a critique of the LRCWA recommendation, not the legal system.

(C) This one is, perhaps, the most superficially tempting of the incorrect answers. (C) has a couple of things going for it. First, it correctly reflects that the passage is about a recommended change. Second, it recognizes that the author does not like the proposed change. The problem with (C) is that while the author doesn't like the recommendation of the LRCWA, he doesn't take the position that it would make things *worse*. The author's problem with the recommendation is that it doesn't go far enough. The last paragraph makes it very clear that the author supports contingency fee agreements; the three reasons given in support of contingency fee agreements "hold for all clients." Currently, there are *no* permitted contingency fees in Western Australia (lines 6-7: "*introducing* contingency fees..."). The disagreement with the recommendation isn't that it would make things worse; it's (mostly) that it wouldn't make things 'better enough,' because not everybody would enjoy the benefits that contingency fee agreements can provide (lines 41-44).

(D) It's hard to say what "significantly" changed means; I could possibly argue that the author believes that the legal system would not be significantly changed under the LRCWA proposal (which can be the only "certain reforms" that (D) means), because only a very select group of clients will be able to take advantage of the uplift fee agreements (lines 42-48). On the other hand, I could argue that opening up the system to allow contingency fee agreements, even in just a small set of circumstances, *is* a "significant" change. One problem with (D), then, is that it's so vague, it's hard to say exactly what it means. The bigger problem is that even if it's true that the passage says what (D) claims, it just isn't the main point. The main point is to describe the proposal, and to outline why it's not a particularly good one.

(E) Correct. All of the general terms of this answer choice match up to the specific content of the passage. We have a suggested reform – the LRCWA's recommendation (both a "reform" (change) and a "recommended" one – it has not been put in place) – and we also have a critical evaluation of it. In fact, the passage is a "critical" evaluation of the suggested reform in more than one sense – it is both fault-finding and evaluative. Whether or not the wording of this answer choice is what I expected, the content is spot-on; the passage does two things – tells us what the recommendation is, and tells us what's wrong with it.

Afterthoughts: This is a pretty straightforward Main Point question. For the most part, it's just a matter of being careful and watching out for the choices that are in the ballpark, for instance, don't get lazy and select (B) just because it mentions 'shortcomings' – pay attention to the details and realize that the passage isn't about the shortcomings of the current legal system; it's about the shortcomings of the proposal.

24. Forethoughts: I know right where to go with this question – the third paragraph talks about problems with the uplift fee agreements. Two specific problems are cited: First, the lawyer won't know the financial circumstances of the client; second, the lawyer won't necessarily know how much the case is going to cost. Those two factors are relevant, because under the proposal, the lawyer must be satisfied that the client can't afford the cost of the litigation via a traditional fee structure (e.g. hourly rates). So, I'm looking for reference to one of those two things.

> (A) Remember the key phrase from the question: "…given by the passage as a reason…" It may be true that it's difficult to predict how long a trial will last (usually not, though; judges like to know what's going on with their calendars, and at a pretrial conference or by written submission, they will ask the lawyers how long the trial is expected to last. The responses by the lawyers are pretty reliable – they know how many witnesses they'll have, how long they'll spend with them, etc.) That's neither here nor there, though; the key point is that the *passage* doesn't tell us that trials are of unpredictable durations, so this can't be the right answer. Keep your answers confined to the information in the passage.
>
> (B) This one is even more likely to be true than (A), but again, it's not in the passage. The passage states that lawyers would be required to investigate the potential client's financial circumstances, and it's quite likely that some of them would resist that investigation. And yes, that would be a problem, because if the lawyer couldn't satisfy himself that the clients would not be able to afford the legal fees in the absence of a recovery, then the lawyer cannot enter into an uplift fee agreement in accordance with the recommendation. Again, though, none of that matters, because <u>the passage doesn't state</u> that some clients wouldn't wish to reveal detailed information about their finances.
>
> (C) Correct. The passage is clear: The cost of litigation depends on "factors that may change as the case unfolds." (lines 37-39). Whether you think this is more or less of a reason than those in (A) and (B) is irrelevant – we're not looking for the *best* reason; we're looking for the one that's mentioned in the passage.
>
> (D) This one is sneaky. It *does* appear in the passage – the recommendation is that uplift fees be used only as a last resort (23-26). So what's wrong with (D)? It doesn't answer the question! We're looking for a reason that lawyer's would have trouble determining whether a prospective client is "qualified to enter into an uplift agreement." The recommendation that uplift agreements should be a last resort has nothing to do with how easy it would be for the lawyer to determine whether or not the potential client would qualify under the recommendation.

Yes, you have to read the passage carefully...but you also have to read the question carefully, too.

(E) This is possibly true, but, like (D), has nothing to do with whether or not lawyers would have a difficult time determining whether or not prospective clients qualify for the uplift agreements. I would say the passage sort of implies that (E) is true (lines 32-35), but, again, it doesn't really matter. Even if (E) is true, and even if (E) is construed to be given by the passage, it doesn't answer the question asked.

Afterthoughts: This is a good question to illustrate a potential trap that usually shows up in the Logical Reasoning section – sometimes, an answer choice that is *true* can be *wrong*. The issue isn't whether any given answer choice is a true statement; it's whether it answers the question asked. In the Logical Reasoning section, this seems to turn up most often in assumption questions. A wrong answer may be a true statement, or at least consistent with the argument, just not an assumption that's required by the argument, or sufficient to draw the conclusion of the argument. So the lesson of question 24 is that it's not only important to read the *passage* carefully; it's also important to read the *question* carefully. If you read both the passage and the question carefully here, you should end up at (C). It's the one that's both in the passage *and* addresses the question asked.

25. Forethoughts: By now, you probably know that I love the Reading Comp questions that direct me to a particular portion of the passage, as this one does. However, this one, in my view, is unusually challenging for a question that points us directly to just a couple of specific lines. So, what does "gaining disproportionately from awards of damages" mean? The key to the uplift agreements is that they tie the fee to the lawyer's usual fee, regardless of the amount of damages. So, if the agreed-upon increase is 50% of the lawyer's fee, then a lawyer who makes $300/hour for hourly work will make $450/hour if the result of the case is a success. He won't gain "disproportionately" from an award of damages, because his fee is not tied into the amount of damages. The lawyer, for instance, does the same amount of work whether he gets a $100,000 verdict or a $1,000,000 verdict. Under the uplift agreement, his fee would be the same. But if his compensation were a percentage of the award, then he would make 10 times as much for the same amount of work if he gets the million dollar verdict. That sounds like the "disproportionate" gain.

(A) By definition (as I understand the terms), there is no danger of an attorney's fees being worth more than the monetary value of the services, under a traditional contingency fee agreement. If the lawyer gets, say, 30%, then the client gets most of the money. The pure monetary value of the lawyer's services, if he wins a $100,000 case, is $100,000; the client will keep most (70%) of it. The client will never have to pay more than the $100,000, or anything close to it.

(B) Correct, though maybe not easy to see. Let's go back to our hypothetical lawyer in (A), who gets $30,000 for obtaining a $100,000 verdict (30%). Let's further assume that he put 100 hours into the case. So, he's earned $300/hour for his efforts, or in the words of (B), for "the professional services rendered and the amount of the risk assumed." The risk was that he put in those 300 hours, and if he hadn't won the case, he wouldn't have received a dime. So, he's made 30% "of the total amount awarded," and we'd consider that "reasonable compensation," because $300 is a reasonable hourly wage for a lawyer.

Now, let's say that the defendant had been remorseful, or worried that a verdict against him might be huge, so instead, the lawyer made a 1-hour phone call and the defendant agreed to settle the case for the same $100,000. Now, the lawyer still makes 30%, but it translates to $30,000/hour, an amount that most would *not* consider "reasonable compensation" for one hour of work and almost no risk assumed. This is the situation that the uplift fees are trying to prevent; under the proposal, the lawyer would have made his hourly rate + some percentage – probably less than 1% of the total damages awarded (or agreed-upon, in the case of a settlement). Having done almost no work, a fee of, say, 1% (or less) would be considered more reasonable, with 99+% of the award going to the party that suffered the damages that brought about the case. Under this model, the lawyer might legitimately earn his way up to 30% of the damages, but only by putting a lot of hours into the case.

(C) This is almost a philosophical answer about perception and reality. The question is about lawyers "gaining disproportionately" (reality), not about whether clients *consider* the award "fair" (perception). If the concern was about client perception (and therefore, presumably, client satisfaction), it probably would have been worded a lot differently, e.g. "This restriction is intended to promote public confidence in the legal profession by ensuring that hourly rates are *perceived as fair*…"

(D) This is a poor answer choice. The phrase in question concerns something that the recommendation is intended to *prevent*. ("…designed to prevent lawyers from gaining disproportionately…") The recommendation is not intended to prevent a lawyer receiving a higher payment in a successful case; *any* contingency fee would ensure that the lawyer gets paid more for a successful case. The passage tells us that in an unsuccessful contingency fee case, the client gets *nothing* (lines 7-8). So it would make no sense to say that a recommendation for a contingency fee structure would be designed to *prevent* a lawyer from making more in a successful case. That's what contingency fee cases are all about – the lawyer gets paid more (only gets paid *at all*) if he wins.

(E) The jury (or the judge, in certain cases) compensates the plaintiff for the loss suffered by the defendant's actions. If the defendant breached a contract, the jury awards the plaintiff the money that he lost because of the defendant's breach. If the defendant injured the plaintiff through negligent conduct, the jury awards the plaintiff for his medical bills, lost wages, pain & suffering, etc. The jury doesn't "intend" for any particular *percentage* of the award to go to the attorney. Moreover, a traditional contingency fee agreement could result in a higher or a lower fee than an hourly rate, or an "uplift" agreement, depending on how many hours a lawyer has to sink into the case.

For instance, let's go back to our lawyer who makes $100,000 for his client, getting 30% as a contingency fee. If the lawyer's rate for hourly rate is $300/hour, and the "uplift" fee is his hourly rate + 1/3 (i.e. $400/hour), is the uplift fee more than his traditional contingency fee award, or less? The answer is, we have no way of knowing. If he knocks the case out in 50 hours, he's made $600/hour ($30,000 divided by 50 hours), and the uplift structure cuts his hourly wage. But if he had to spend 200 hours on the case, he would have made $150/hour ($30,000 divided by 200 hours), and the uplift structure would actually *increase* his hourly wage. A lawyer's hourly wage under a traditional contingency fee structure is very unpredictable, because you never know how many hours you'll have to put into a case.

Afterthoughts: The key to this one might be "proportionately." The question of proportion implies more than one thing; it's a comparison. So the obvious question in analyzing the phrase "gaining proportionately from awards of damages" is "disproportionate to *what*?!" In a traditional contingency, by definition, the lawyer's money isn't disproportionate to the client's money; it's a straight percentage. So what's it disproportionate to? If it's not the money earned for the client, it's got to be the work done by the lawyer. The LRCWA's recommendation suggests that there should be a proportionality between the work done and the share of the recovery – the "reasonable compensation for services rendered" and the "higher portion of the total amount rewarded." I found this to be the most challenging of the Reading Comp questions from Test 60, but your mileage may vary.

26. Forethoughts: Having worked through a number of questions before this one, I'm pretty familiar by now with what the passage says about the LRCWA's recommended limitations. The main recommendations are that contingency fee agreements 1) be limited to uplift agreements (where the fee can expressed as a percentage of the lawyer's hourly rate (lines 12-17)); 2) be used only when some other fee arrangement cannot be used (lines 24-26); and 3) be used only when the lawyer determines that the client wouldn't be able to pay his hourly fee if the case loses (lines 27-29)(which is really more of a continuation of 2)). So, I'm hoping to see something that sounds like it would fit

under one of those three possibilities; if not, I'll have to look harder at a couple of the answer choices.

(A) This doesn't fit into one of the categories outlines in the Forethoughts. I do remember that there's a bit about diligence and commitment; in fact, it's the last line of the passage. But the reference to diligence and commitment isn't that it should be used "only when it's reasonable" to think that those things will transpire. That part of the passage is just outlining the benefits of contingency fee agreements. If the lawyer stands to make more money if he succeeds, then the general assumption is that he's going to be extremely diligent and committed.

(B) This is also incorrect, and, moreover, seems inconsistent with the passage. The recommendation is that the lawyer's fees will be his base hourly rate plus some percentage of that rate. So if the case is a winner, then whether or not the client is awarded enormous damages, the lawyer would receive the same amount. In other words, it should be irrelevant to the LRCWA how much the client receives. Why does it matter whether the client gets $100,000 or $20,000,000 if the lawyer's fee is $10,000 (or whatever other number you want to make up for the hourly fees)? If anything, clients that are "likely" to recover enormous damages are good fits for contingency fee agreements (including the uplift agreements), because (assuming they win, as they're likely to do) they'll be able to pay their legal fees after the case resolves. If a client is awarded only minimal damages, he might not be able to pay the lawyer an hourly fee even after receiving the money from the case.

(C) This is getting closer, but it's still wrong. It's closer, because the recommendation does reference the lawyer's belief about whether the client could afford the fees if the case is unsuccessful. The problem with (C) is that it doesn't quite go far enough. The recommendation isn't that uplift fees should be used if the lawyer "*is not certain*" that the client would be able to pay his fees if the case is unsuccessful; it's that they should *only* be used if the lawyer is satisfied that the client would not be able to pay his fees if the case is unsuccessful (27-29). "Uncertain" means that the lawyer would not know; but the recommendation requires that the lawyer investigate until he *does* know (or, at least, is "satisfied") that the contingency fee is the only way he's going to get paid.

(D) Correct. Lines 24-26. Contingency fees are to be a "last resort" to be used when all means of avoiding them have been exhausted. Which is another way of saying that they're not to be used if there's a practicable alternative. This is one of the of the specific recommendations I was looking for, which helps me avoid being distracted by (C), which may fairly be construed as a tempting wrong answer.

(E) Another "close but not quite" answer. The recommendation isn't that the lawyer must be sure the client will be able to cover the lawyer's fees if he wins; it's that the lawyer has to be sure that the client *won't* be able to cover the fees if he *doesn't* win. That is, his only hope of paying the bills is to win a sufficient award, but the lawyer doesn't have to be "reasonably sure" that will happen. A lawyer who isn't reasonably sure that will happen might still take a longshot case, especially if there was an outside chance at recovering really big damages. He could just price the unlikelihood of recovery into his "uplift" fee. For instance, say there's a case that will probably lose, but there's a 20% chance that it will result in a $10,000,000 award. The lawyer might take that case and say, "You owe me nothing if we lose, but if we win, you have to pay triple my normal fee." That's a potentially legitimate use of the uplift fee. It gives the client a chance at representation and a big award, where he wouldn't have been able to afford a lawyer without the contingency, and the lawyer can set the "uplift" fairly high (a 200% bonus), to allow for the probability that he'll lose the case. There's no need at all for the lawyer to be "reasonably sure" that a big award will be forthcoming.

Afterthoughts: Two of the wrong answers strike me as tempting – (C) and (E). This is a good question for illustrating the benefit of predicting what the right answer might look like before you start looking at the answer choices. The question asks about the report's recommendations for contingency-fee agreements, so take a few seconds and see what those recommendations are. Then when you see an answer choice that matches up to one of them, you're less likely to get caught up in the doubletalk of the other answers. If you had trouble separating (C), (D), and (E), another tip that can be helpful is this – analyze the least confusing of the answer choices. (C) and (E) are considerably more convoluted than (D). So focus on (D) – you're more likely to able to determine whether it's right or wrong, because it's more understandable. And it will be faster to analyze, for the same reason. If you focus on (D), comparing it to the passage (lines 24-26), then you'll probably be fairly confident that it's correct – and that means that you won't have to worry about untangling (C) and (E).

27. Forethoughts: The first thing I need to understand is what the author's criticism of the recommendations is. There seem to be two general objections – 1) investigating the client's financial situation would be very burdensome; and 2) by limiting the availability of contingency fee agreements, the LRCWA proposed to keep contingency fee agreements unavailable to many potential clients. So now I'm looking for something that would weaken one of those two objections.

(A) This doesn't fit either of the categories of criticism by the author. It's completely irrelevant to investigating the client's finances, and it doesn't address the proposal's limited availability; it just states something we'd expect about uplift agreements – their presence makes it more likely that the least well-off clients will file lawsuits, because they're a type of contingency fee, and without a contingency fee, those clients wouldn't be able to afford an attorney.doesn't fit either of the categories of criticism by the author. It's completely irrelevant to investigating the client's finances, and it doesn't address the proposal's limited availability; it just states something we'd expect about uplift agreements – their presence makes it more likely that the least well-off clients will file lawsuits, because they're a type of contingency fee, and without a contingency fee, those clients wouldn't be able to afford an attorney.

(B) Correct. The criticism is that the recommendation would be "onerous" (burdensome) (line 36), because lawyers would have to investigate the case, but "also the financial circumstances of the client…" (B) weakens that argument, because it says that the lawyers in the state are *already* investigating their clients' financial circumstances in potentially complex cases. If that's true, the proposal isn't burdensome; it just requires lawyers to do something they're doing anyway.

(C) This answer choice can be construed as either irrelevant or "beyond the scope" of the question. The author of the passage is criticizing the recommendation of the LRCWA – he doesn't think it's a good recommendation. A weakening of his criticism would show (as in (B), above) that the proposal is not as bad as the author thinks. Whether or not it will be implemented does not address whether or not the proposal is as bad as the author thinks it is.

(D) This answer choice does not weaken the criticism, because the author's criticism has nothing to do with the amount of the fees charged by lawyers. The criticism is about the limited availability of the uplift agreements, and the burden inherent with investigating clients' finances.

(E) Much like (D), this does not address any of the author's criticisms. Whether they use uplift fees more often, less often, or just as often as other contingency fee agreements has nothing to do with whether or not the author's specific criticisms of the recommendations are justified or not.

Afterthoughts: Remember to stay specific and answer the question that's being asked. Answer choice (D), for instance, answers a *potential* criticism that somebody *might* have about the uplift fees. Maybe someone would argue that the "agreed upon additional percentage" in the uplift fee isn't fair. Why should a winning client in a contingency fee case pay more than the winning client under an hourly agreement? (D) would weak *that* criticism by showing that they're actually not paying all that much more. The reason that's not good enough here is that it's not an argument that was made in the passage. The key to the Reading Comp section is specificity. The question asks about the "*author's* criticism." Keep that first and foremost in your mind, and you'll be able to avoid the wrong answers here.

Afterward

Obviously(?) one could write more than a page and a half on any given LSAT question, but if a practical book is to mirror a student's thought process, then to some extent, it has to be streamlined. It's the LSAT; I can't give you ten minutes' worth of things to think about when you have less than a minute and a half per question. But I've tried to put in all the most important stuff and leave out the least important stuff.

And now, a plea from the author. If I told you how much time went into this book, you'd throw up. I've kept the price low, and intentionally or not, it sort of became a labor of love. If you've gotten something out of it, and you're wondering how you could ever repay me...burn this copy and take your LSAT secrets to the grave. I'm aiming at a niche market here, and you're on your way to a great new career as a lawyer; let the next future law student cut me another check. Of course, you have a perfect *right* to resell it (that's the First Sale Doctrine; for more information, sign up for copyright law when you hit year two of your law school career); I'm just saying if you wanted to help a first-time author out.

And if you DIDN'T get anything out of this book, first, I apologize. Second, that kind of makes it even worse to resell it, don't you think? How could you foist such a horrible book on an unsuspecting buyer?!

On your way to becoming a lawyer, three things are going to be pretty unpleasant – The LSAT, your first year finals (especially the first semester), and the bar exam. Soon, you'll have one of the three knocked out. And remember – Law school gets a lot better after the first year. So hang in there.

Hope this helped.

About the Author

Dan F. Oakes was born and raised and lives in Southern California. After working as, among other things, a journalist and a teacher, he took the LSAT on a whim and his 99th percentile score got him into the UCLA School of Law, from which he subsequently graduated and became an attorney. His strong interest in writing and his passion for teaching led him to the field of LSAT test prep, and he has helped hundreds of students improve their LSAT scores en route to achieving their own dreams of become law students. He knows a lot more about the LSAT after teaching it than he ever did when he took it.